THE YEAR YOU WERE BORN

1940

A fascinating book about the year 1940 with information on History of Britain, Events of the year UK, Adverts of 1940, Cost of living, Births, Sporting events, Book publications, Movies, Music, World events and People in power.

INDEX

HISTORY OF BRITAIN IN 1940

There was a mood of tension in the air that bright morning in the summer of 1940, as the military personnel, scientific experts and government officers gathered at the top of the cliff overlooking the Solent estuary in Hampshire. Next to this distinguished group stood a row of 10 large Scammell petrol tankers, from each of which stretched a long pipe, snaking down the 30-foot-high cliff, across the shoreline and out into the sea. At a given signal, the valves on the 10 petrol tankers were opened, and almost immediately the pipes began to deliver oil into the water at a rate of 12 tonnes an hour.

What happened next profoundly impressed the gathering. A series of flares and sodium pellets were fired into the sea. As they ignited the oil, a gigantic wall of flame raged up from the surface with such intensity that it seemed as if the sea itself had begun to boil, while thick black smoke climbed thousands of feet above the fiery barrage.

The remarkable sight of the burning sea sent a wave of excitement through the military and the government. Why? Well this experiment, held at Titchfield on 24 August 1940, took place at a moment when the fate of Britain hung in the balance. With most of western Europe now under the control of Hitler's Reich, an imminent German invasion seemed inevitable.

In the skies over southern England, the RAF fought heroically to stop the Luftwaffe gaining air superiority, one of the essential conditions for any seaborne assault launched by Hitler. But now the British authorities felt that they might have another weapon that could be highly effective against an invader. One of those who witnessed the Titchfield trial, Vice Admiral Sir Geoffrey Arbuthnot, called it "an outstanding success", adding: "I do not believe that any landing forces would attempt to pierce the flames even if the force were aware of the width of fire."

Yet, for all the combustible inspiration it provided, the burning sea trial was hardly unique in the summer of 1940. Britain's determination to resist a German assault could be seen in everything from the creation of new types of bombs to the mass installation of road blocks. With the invasion looming, Britain bristled with a fortress mentality.

This was a land where signposts were removed from every road, where 18,000 pillboxes were built and where beaches were protected by miles of barbed wire.

The idea of Britain as a well-prepared nation, ready for a German attack, runs counter to the usual narrative of 1940. According to the myths about this period, Britain was in a state of ill-defended, poorly equipped weakness, thanks to years of complacency from pre-war governments.

This chronic feebleness was supposedly symbolised by the laughable inadequacy of the Home Guard, subsequently immortalised in the TV comedy Dad's Army, whose weaponry was said to be as woeful as the calibre of its recruits. According to this account, Britain was only saved from inevitable defeat and subjugation by the courage of the Fighter Command pilots.

There is another fashionable argument which holds that the Germans were never serious about invasion, which meant that Britain survived, not through her own efforts, but simply because of the enemy's hesitations. There is no doubt that Hitler was ambivalent about a direct attack on southern England, partly because of his fears about marine operations. "On land I feel like a lion, but at sea I am a coward," he once said. Other factors that fuelled his doubts were his admiration for the British empire and his belief that London would be forced by military realities to negotiate.

Nevertheless, after the fall of France in mid-June, the German High Command embarked on extensive preparations for an invasion, especially the creation of a vast, makeshift fleet of barges to carry the invasion force, which would ultimately comprise 260,000 troops, to the southern English coast. In a series of military conferences from early July 1940, the Germans worked out in great detail the invasion plan, to be called Operation Sea lion, even down to the number of guard dogs that would take part in the landings.

But the belief that Britain was hopelessly ill-prepared to tackle the invasion threat is a romantic fallacy that downplays the dynamism of Churchill's government and the public. The Finest Hour belonged not just to the RAF but to the wider nation. Contrary to the image of institutionalised chaos in 1940, British military and political officialdom was tough, resilient, well organised and resourceful. The political ruthlessness that brought Winston Churchill to power in early May 1940, when the Tory party rebelled against the ineffectual leadership of Neville Chamberlain, was reflected in a host of other initiatives, like incarceration of all enemy aliens and political extremists, the destruction of the French fleet at Oran to stop it falling into the hands of the enemy and the control of the entire German spy network in Britain after turning several agents.

In the same ruthless spirit, General Edmund Ironside was sacked as the commander-in-chief of home forces in late July 1940, despite his popularity with the public, because Churchill regarded him as too pessimistic and defensive. One of his critics, the military historian Basil Liddell-Hart, even described Ironside as "gaga". His replacement, the Ulsterman General Alan Brooke, was a figure of much greater natural authority.

The British were also far more efficient than is often recognised. A host of massive logistical exercises were carried out with barely a single hitch, like the shipment of all the Bank of England's gold reserves to Canada, the evacuation of schoolchildren from London, and the transfer of national art treasures to remote hiding places.

Similarly, British military defences were stronger than historical mythology suggests. The Royal Navy, which would have had the primary responsibility of defending the Channel, had 10 times as many destroyers as Hitler's Kriegsmarine, while the regular army had an overall force of some 1.3 million men in uniform at the end of July 1940.

That total excludes the Home Guard, which has long been subject to mockery. But actually the arming of this force, far from being an embarrassment, is a graphic illustration of how successfully Britain prepared to counter Sea lion. It is true that in the early days of May 1940, just after the War Office had announced the formation of the Local Defence Volunteers, as the Home Guard was originally known, the weapons for the individual units could hardly have been more primitive. Muskets, blunderbusses, swords, truncheons, golf clubs, crossbows and even chair legs all found their way into the LDVs' arsenal. One unit in Lancashire was equipped with Snyder rifles held in Manchester Zoo and last used during the Indian Mutiny of 1857.

But this picture had dramatically changed by August 1940, thanks to the import of weapons from America, the bulk of which were 615,000 M1917 rifles, dating from the First World War. These arms are often described as poor and antiquated, but they were just as good as the standard issue Lee Enfield's used by the regular army. Indeed, in ballistic terms, they were superior to the Lee Enfield's because their .30 calibre rounds had a flatter trajectory. One sniper instructor, Clifford Shore, described the M1917 as "probably the most accurate rifle I ever used" and a "splendid weapon".

The same was true of other American weapons supplied to the Home Guard, blowing apart the Dad's Army caricature of pitchforks and broom handles. A total of 25,000 Browning Automatic Rifles, with a rate of fire of 500 rounds per minute, and 22,000 Browning water-cooled machine guns found their way to Home Guard units before September 1940, by which time more than 900,000 volunteers were in uniform.

Less orthodox weapons than the M1917 and Lee Enfield rifles also played their role in Britain's land defences. These included: the Self-Igniting Phosphorous (SIP) grenade made by the Midlands firm of Albright and Wilson, which was essentially a half-pint bottle filled with an inflammable mixture of white phosphorous, benzene, and crude rubber; the anti-tank Number 74 Grenade, colloquially known as the 'Sticky Bomb', made up of a spherical glass flask filled with nitro-glycerine and attached to a wooden handle, giving the weapon a resemblance to a toffee apple; and the McNaughton mine, an underground pipe, filled with explosives, that could be placed under bridges, roads and railways to halt the advance of the enemy.

Far more deadly were the poisonous gas weapons that Britain planned to deploy against the German invader, in defiance of the Geneva protocols on the conduct of war. Some were appalled at the idea of such illegality. Major General Desmond Anderson of the army's Imperial General Staff argued that such a move would be "a departure from our principles and traditions", which would prompt "some of us to begin to wonder whether it really mattered which side won".

But neither the chiefs of staff nor Churchill had any time for such sensitivities when Britain's survival was at stake. "We should not hesitate to contaminate our beaches with gas if this would be to our advantage. We have the right to do what we like with our own territory," said Churchill. Accordingly, the British armed forces were equipped to use gas, both on land and from the air.

By the summer of 1940, the army had 10 companies that were trained to handle chemical weapons. Their substantial stores were made up of 25,000 shells filled with mustard gas, 15,000 ground bombs, and 1,000 chemical mines, as well as 10 'Bulk Contamination Vehicles' and 950 projectors that could fire chemical-filled drums. Meanwhile, Bomber Command had 16 squadrons that were designated for duty in either spraying gas or dropping chemical bombs on the enemy. By the autumn of 1940, Britain's stock of chemical weapons amounted to 13,000 tonnes.

The country also had huge reserves of petroleum, which explains why the government was willing to pursue such fuel-hungry experiments as the marine flame barrage.

Supplies of petrol were also used in the development of innovative land weapons against the invader, like the static flame trap, which consisted of an oil tank connected to a network of perforated steel pipes, laid by the road, which could let off huge jets of fire at the enemy once ignited. There was also the lethal 'flame fougasse', a barrel full of an oil mixture that, when detonated, could cover a large area with burning liquid. "Nothing could have lived in it," said Fred Hilton, a Lancastrian soldier who witnessed one demonstration of this weapon.

In mid-September 1940, just when German preparations for Operation Sea lion were meant to have been completed, British propaganda brilliantly exploited these experiments in petroleum warfare to heighten apprehension among the Reich's planners and seaborne forces. This was done by using intelligence networks on the continent to spread rumours about charred corpses of German soldiers being washed up on the beaches of both sides of the Channel. Such rumours carried a degree of credibility because large numbers of German troops had indeed been burnt in heavy RAF bombing raids on the enemy barges in the Channel ports. British radio broadcasts and more than a million leaflets added to the fear by giving mock English language lessons for the putative invaders. "See how well the captain burns," was one sarcastic phrase in this British material.

All this activity, from the propaganda to the RAF bombing raids, from the continuing resilience of Fighter Command to the growing strength of the beach defences, cast severe doubts in the minds of Hitler and his military chiefs about Operation Sea lion. Faced with all the evidence of such a determined foe, the gamble seemed too great. On 17th September 1940, Hitler announced an indefinite postponement of Operation Sea lion. Officially, the invasion plans remained in place until the spring of 1941, partly to keep Britain on the defensive, but after September, Hitler never had any intention of implementing them. Thwarted in the west, his thoughts turned to the east, with ultimately disastrous consequences.

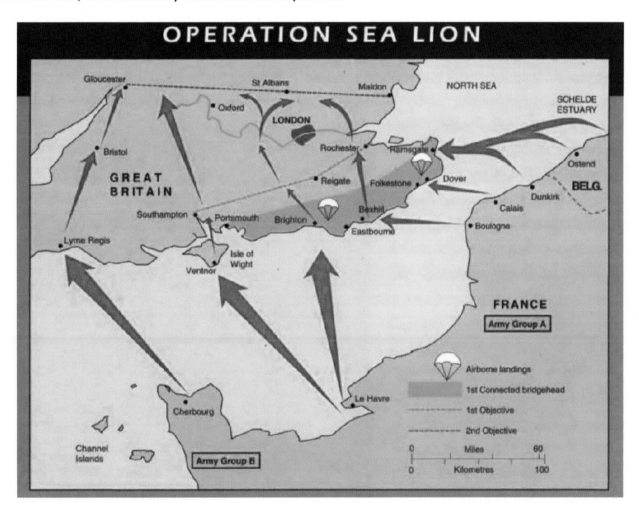

UK EVENTS OF 1940

January

1st | World War II: Britain calls up 2,000,000 19- to 27-year-olds for military service.

3rd | Unity Mitford, daughter of David Freeman-Mitford, 2nd Baron Redesdale, and fervent admirer of Adolf Hitler, having attempted suicide, returns to England from Germany (via Switzerland); she is carried down the gangplank of the cross-channel ferry at Folkestone on a stretcher.

5th | Oliver Stanley replaces Leslie Hore-Belisha as Secretary of State for War.

8th | The first commodity to be controlled was gasoline. On the 8th January 1940, bacon, butter and sugar were rationed. This was followed by successive ration schemes for meat, tea, jam, biscuits, breakfast cereals, cheese, eggs, lard, milk and canned and dried fruit. Fresh vegetables and fruit were not rationed but supplies were limited. Many people grew their own vegetables, greatly encouraged by the highly successful 'digging for victory' motivational campaign. Most controversial was bread; it was not rationed until after the war ended, but the "national loaf" of wholemeal bread replaced the ordinary white variety, to the distaste of most housewives who found it mushy, grey and easy to blame for digestion problems. Fish was not rationed but price increased considerably as the war progressed.

9th | World War II: liner Dunbar Castle of the Union Castle Line hits a mine in the English Channel and sinks with the loss of 9 men.

17th | A wave of freezing weather afflicting most of Europe leads to the River Thames freezing for the first time since 1888.

18th | Explosion at Waltham Abbey Royal Gunpowder Mills kills five people.

26th | British battleship HMS Barham is torpedoed by a U-boat but suffers only minor damage.

February

3rd | A Heinkel He 111 bomber is the first German plane shot down over England.

16th | Altmark Incident: Royal Navy destroyer HMS Cossack (F03) pursues German tanker Altmark into the neutral waters of Jøssingfjord in southwestern Norway and frees the 290 British seamen held aboard.

HMS Cossack was a Tribal-class destroyer named after the Cossack people of the Russian and Ukrainian steppe. She became famous for the boarding of the German supply ship Altmark in Norwegian waters, and the associated rescue of sailors originally captured by the Admiral Graf Spee. She was torpedoed by U-563 on the 23rd October 1941, and sank 4 days later, on the 27th October.

March

1st Frisch–Peierls memorandum: Otto Frisch and Rudolf Peierls, at this time working at the University of Birmingham, calculate that an atomic bomb could be produced using very much less enriched uranium than has previously been supposed, making it a practical proposition.

3rd RMS Queen Elizabeth makes her maiden voyage on delivery from Clydebank to New York.

March

11th Rationing of meat introduced.

16th First civilian casualty of bombing in the UK, on Orkney.

29th Metal security threads added to £1 notes to prevent forgeries. A security thread is a security feature of many banknotes to protect against counterfeiting, consisting of a thin ribbon that is threaded through the note's paper. Usually, the ribbon runs vertically, and is "woven" into the paper, so that it at some places emerges on the front side and at the remaining places at the rear side of the paper. Usually, it is made of metal foil, but sometimes of plastic. Often, it has some text or numbers (e.g., the denomination) engraved.

31st 33 fascist sympathisers, including Oswald Mosley, are interned.

April

1st British Overseas Airways Corporation (BOAC) was the British state-owned airline created in 1939 by the merger of Imperial Airways and British Airways Ltd. Its first flight was on the 1st April. It continued operating overseas services throughout World War II. After the passing of the Civil Aviation Act 1946, European and South American services passed to two further state-owned airlines, British European Airways (BEA) and British South American Airways (BSAA). BOAC absorbed BSAA in 1949, but BEA continued to operate British domestic and European routes for the next quarter century. A 1971 Act of Parliament merged BOAC and BEA, effective from the 31st March 1974, forming today's British Airways.

April

5th | Neville Chamberlain declares in a public speech that Hitler has "missed the bus".

9th | British campaign in Norway commences following Operation Weserübung, the German invasion of neutral Denmark and Norway. Operation Weserübung was the code name for Germany's assault on Denmark and Norway during the Second World War and the opening operation of the Norwegian Campaign. The name comes from the German for "Operation Weser-Exercise", the Weser being a German river.

12th | The British occupation of the Faroe Islands in World War II, also known as Operation Valentine, was implemented immediately following the German invasion of Denmark and Norway. It was a small component of the roles of Nordic countries in World War II. On the 12th April 1940, the United Kingdom occupied the strategically important Faroe Islands to forestall a German invasion. British troops left shortly after the end of the war.

23rd | The War Budget sees the introduction of Purchase Tax and an increase in tobacco duties. Purchase Tax was a tax levied between 1940 and 1973 on the wholesale value of luxury goods sold in the United Kingdom. Introduced on 21 October 1940, with the stated aim of reducing the wastage of raw materials during World War II, it was initially set at a rate of 33⅓%.

The tax was subsequently set at differing rates dependent upon individual items' degree of "luxury" as determined by the government of the day.

In connection with the accession of the UK to the European Economic Community (EU) Purchase Tax was abolished on 2 April 1973 and replaced by Value Added Tax (VAT), initially set at a rate of 10%, which was shortly afterwards reduced to 8%.

May

2nd | Last British and French troops evacuated from Norway following failure in the Norwegian Campaign. The Norwegian campaign was the attempted Allied liberation of Norway from Nazi Germany during the early stages of World War II and directly following the German invasion and occupation of the Norwegian mainland and government. It took place from the 9th April 1940, until the 10th June 1940. The Allied campaign did not succeed, and it resulted in the fleeing of King Haakon VII along with the remainder of the royal family to Great Britain.

7th | The Norway Debate, sometimes called the Narvik Debate, was a momentous debate in the British House of Commons during the Second World War from 7th to 9th May 1940. It has been called the most far-reaching parliamentary debate of the twentieth century. At the end of the second day, a vote held by the members resulted in a drastically reduced government majority. This led, on the 10th May, to Neville Chamberlain's resignation as Prime Minister and the replacement of his war ministry by a broadly-based coalition government which, under Winston Churchill, governed the United Kingdom until the end of the war in Europe in May 1945.

9th | In private discussions, Viscount Halifax rules himself out as successor to Chamberlain in favour of Winston Churchill.

May

10th Neville Chamberlain resigns as Prime Minister, and is replaced by Winston Churchill with a coalition war ministry. The Churchill war ministry was the United Kingdom's coalition government for most of the Second World War from the 10th May 1940 to the 23rd May 1945. It was led by Winston Churchill, who was appointed Prime Minister by King George VI following the resignation of Arthur Neville Chamberlain in the aftermath of the Norway Debate.

At the outset, Churchill formed a five-man War Cabinet which included Chamberlain as Lord President of the Council, Clement Attlee as Lord Privy Seal and later as Deputy Prime Minister, Viscount Halifax as Foreign Secretary and Arthur Greenwood as a Minister without Portfolio. Although the original war cabinet was limited to five members, in practice they were augmented by the service chiefs who attended the majority of meetings. The cabinet changed in size and membership as the war progressed but there were significant additions later in 1940 when it was increased to eight after Churchill, Attlee and Greenwood were joined by Ernest Bevin as Minister of Labour and National Service; Anthony Eden as Foreign Secretary – replacing Halifax, who was sent to Washington D.C. as ambassador to the United States; Lord Beaverbrook as Minister of Aircraft Production; Sir Kingsley Wood as Chancellor of the Exchequer and Sir John Anderson as Lord President of the Council – replacing Chamberlain who died in November.

13th Winston Churchill makes his famous "I have nothing to offer you but blood, toil, tears, and sweat" speech to the House of Commons.

14th Queen Wilhelmina of the Netherlands and her government are evacuated to London using HMS Hereward following the German invasion of the Low Countries.

14th Recruitment begins for a home defence force – the Local Defence Volunteers. The Home Guard (initially Local Defence Volunteers or LDV) was an armed citizen militia supporting the British Army during the Second World War. Operational from 1940 to 1944, the Home Guard had 1.5 million local volunteers otherwise ineligible for military service, such as those who were too young or too old to join the regular armed services (regular military service was restricted to those aged 18 to 41) or those in reserved occupations. Excluding those already in the armed services, the civilian police or civil defence, approximately one in five men were volunteers. Their role was to act as a secondary defence force in case of invasion by the forces of Nazi Germany and other Axis powers.

May

22nd | Parliament passes the Emergency Powers (Defence) Act 1940 giving the government full control over all persons and property.

23rd | The Treachery Act 1940 was an Act of the Parliament of the United Kingdom enacted during World War II to facilitate the prosecution and execution of enemy spies, and suspended after the war and later repealed. The law was passed in the month after Nazi Germany invaded France and Winston Churchill became prime minister (23rd May 1940).

24th | Anglo-French Supreme War Council decides to withdraw all forces under its control from Norway.

26th | The Dunkirk evacuation, code-named Operation Dynamo, also known as the Miracle of Dunkirk, was the evacuation of Allied soldiers during World War II from the beaches and harbour of Dunkirk, in the north of France, between the 26th May and the 4th June 1940. The operation commenced after large numbers of Belgian, British, and French troops were cut off and surrounded by German troops during the six-week long Battle of France. In a speech to the House of Commons, British Prime Minister Winston Churchill called this "a colossal military disaster", saying "the whole root and core and brain of the British Army" had been stranded at Dunkirk and seemed about to perish or be captured. In his "we shall fight on the beaches" speech on the 4th June, he hailed their rescue as a "miracle of deliverance".

28th | May 1940 War Cabinet Crisis: Churchill wins the War Cabinet round to his view that there should be no peace negotiations with Hitler, contrary to the view of his Foreign Secretary, Viscount Halifax.

June

4th | "We Shall Fight on the Beaches" speech delivered by Winston Churchill to the House of Commons of the Parliament of the United Kingdom on the 4th June 1940. This was the second of three major speeches given around the period of the Battle of France; the others are the "Blood, toil, tears, and sweat" speech of 13th May and the "This was their finest hour" speech of 18th June. Events developed dramatically over the five-week period, and although broadly similar in themes, each speech addressed a different military and diplomatic context.

5th | Novelist J. B. Priestley broadcasts his first Sunday evening radio Postscript, "An excursion to hell", on the BBC Home Service, marking the role of the pleasure steamers in the Dunkirk evacuation.

9th | The Commandos also known as British Commandos were formed during the Second World War on the 9th June 1940, following a request from the Prime Minister of the United Kingdom, Winston Churchill, for a force that could carry out raids against German-occupied Europe. Initially drawn from within the British Army from soldiers who volunteered for the Special Service Brigade, the Commandos' ranks would eventually be filled by members of all branches of the British Armed Forces and a number of foreign volunteers from German-occupied countries.

10th | Italy declares war on France and the United Kingdom.

11th | The Western Desert Campaign opens with British forces crossing the Frontier Wire into Italian Libya.

June

12th | Over 10,000 soldiers of the 51st (Highland) Division under General Victor Fortune surrender to Rommel at Saint-Valery-en-Caux.

16th | The Churchill war ministry offers a Franco-British Union to Paul Reynaud, Prime Minister of France, in the hope of preventing France from agreeing to an armistice with Nazi Germany.

17th | RMS Lancastria, serving as a troopship, is bombed and sunk by the Luftwaffe while evacuating British troops and nationals from Saint-Nazaire with the loss of at least 4,000 lives, the largest single UK loss in any World War II event, immediate news of which is suppressed in the British press. Destroyer HMS Beagle (H30) rescues around 600.

18th | Churchill makes his Battle of Britain speech to the House of Commons: "...the Battle of France is over. The Battle of Britain is about to begin... if the British Empire and its Commonwealth last for a thousand years, men will still say, This was their finest hour."

23rd | It was the start of the evacuation of British gold reserves to Canada.

30th | The German occupation of the Channel Islands lasted for most of the Second World War, from the 30th June 1940 until their liberation on the 9th May 1945. The Bailiwick of Jersey and Bailiwick of Guernsey are two British Crown dependencies in the English Channel, near the coast of Normandy. The Channel Islands were the only part of the British Isles to be occupied by the Wehrmacht (German Armed Forces) during the war. Anticipating a swift victory over Britain, the occupiers experimented by using a very gentle approach that set the theme for the next five years. The island authorities adopted a similar attitude, giving rise to accusations of collaboration. However, as time progressed the situation grew gradually worse, ending in near starvation for both occupied and occupiers during the winter of 1944–45.

July

2nd | British-owned SS Arandora Star, carrying civilian internees and POWs of Italian and German origin from Liverpool to Canada, is torpedoed and sunk by German submarine U-47 off northwest Ireland with the loss of around 865 lives.

3rd | Operation Catapult aims to take French navy ships into British control or destroy them to prevent them falling into German hands. Those in port at Plymouth and Portsmouth are boarded and in an attack on Mers-el-Kébir British naval units sink or seize ships of the French fleet anchored in the Algerian ports of Mers El Kébir and Oran.

July

3rd | The following day, Vichy France breaks off diplomatic relations with Britain.

9th | Battle of Britain begins. The Battle of Britain was a military campaign of the Second World War, in which the Royal Air Force defended the United Kingdom against large-scale attacks by Nazi Germany's air force, the Luftwaffe. It has been described as the first major military campaign fought entirely by air forces. The British officially recognise the battle's duration as being from the 9th July until the 31st October 1940, which overlaps the period of large-scale night attacks known as the Blitz that lasted from the 7th September 1940 to 11th May 1941. German historians do not accept this subdivision and regard the battle as a single campaign lasting from July 1940 to June 1941, including the Blitz.

July

19th | Adolf Hitler makes a peace appeal to Britain in an address to the Reichstag. BBC German-language broadcaster Sefton Delmer unofficially rejects it at once and Lord Halifax, British foreign minister, flatly rejects peace terms in a broadcast reply on the 22nd July.

22nd | The Special Operations Executive (SOE) was a British World War II organisation. It was officially formed on the 22nd July 1940 under Minister of Economic Warfare Hugh Dalton, from the amalgamation of three existing secret organisations. Its purpose was to conduct espionage, sabotage and reconnaissance in occupied Europe (and later, also in occupied Southeast Asia) against the Axis powers, and to aid local resistance movements. Few people were aware of SOE's existence. Those who were part of it or liaised with it were sometimes referred to as the "Baker Street Irregulars", after the location of its London headquarters. It was also known as "Churchill's Secret Army" or the "Ministry of Ungentlemanly Warfare". Its various branches, and sometimes the organisation as a whole, were concealed for security purposes behind names such as the "Joint Technical Board" or the "Inter-Service Research Bureau", or fictitious branches of the Air Ministry, Admiralty or War Office. SOE operated in all territories occupied or attacked by the Axis forces, except where demarcation lines were agreed with Britain's principal Allies (the United States and the Soviet Union). It also made use of neutral territory on occasion, or made plans and preparations in case neutral countries were attacked by the Axis. The organisation directly employed or controlled more than 13,000 people, about 3,200 of whom were women. After the war, the organisation was officially dissolved on 15 January 1946. A memorial to SOE's agents was unveiled in October 2009 on the Albert Embankment by Lambeth Palace in London.

August

9th   The Birmingham Blitz was the heavy bombing by the Nazi German Luftwaffe of the city of Birmingham and surrounding towns in central England, beginning on the 9th August 1940 and ending on the 23rd April 1943. It is considered a fraction of the greater Blitz, which was part of the Battle of Britain. Situated in the Midlands, Birmingham, England's most populous British city outside London is an important industrial and manufacturing location. Around 1,852 tons of bombs were dropped on Birmingham, making it the third most heavily bombed city in the United Kingdom in the Second World War, behind only London and Liverpool.

18th   The Hardest Day is a name given to a Second World War air battle fought on the 18th August 1940 during the Battle of Britain between the German Luftwaffe and British Royal Air Force. On this day, the Luftwaffe made an all-out effort to destroy RAF Fighter Command. The air battles that took place on this day were amongst the largest aerial engagements in history to that time. Both sides suffered heavy losses. In the air, the British shot down twice as many Luftwaffe aircraft as they lost. However, many RAF aircraft were destroyed on the ground, equalising the total losses of both sides. Further large and costly aerial battles took place after the 18th August, but both sides lost more aircraft combined on this day than at any other point during the campaign, including the 15th September, the Battle of Britain Day, generally considered the climax of the fighting. For this reason, 18th August 1940 became known as "the Hardest Day" in Britain.

20th   Churchill pays tribute in Parliament to the Royal Air Force fighter crews: "Never in the field of human conflict was so much owed by so many to so few.

September

7th   From the 7th September 1940, London was systematically bombed by the Luftwaffe for 56 of the following 57 days and nights. Most notable was a large daylight attack against London on the 15th September.

The Luftwaffe gradually decreased daylight operations in favour of night attacks to evade attack by the RAF, and the Blitz became a night bombing campaign after October 1940. The Luftwaffe attacked the main Atlantic sea port of Liverpool in the Liverpool Blitz. The North Sea port of Hull, a convenient and easily found target or secondary target for bombers unable to locate their primary targets, suffered the Hull Blitz. Bristol, Cardiff, Portsmouth, Plymouth, Southampton and Swansea were also bombed, as were the industrial cities of Birmingham, Belfast, Coventry, Glasgow, Manchester and Sheffield. More than 40,000 civilians were killed by Luftwaffe bombing during the war, almost half of them in the capital, where more than a million houses were destroyed or damaged.

15th   RAF command claims victory over the Luftwaffe in the Battle of Britain; this day is thereafter known as "Battle of Britain Day".

17th   Hitler postpones Operation Sea Lion, the planned German invasion of Britain, indefinitely.

18th   SS City of Benares is torpedoed by German submarine U-48 in the Atlantic with the loss of 248 of the 406 on board, including child evacuees bound for Canada. The sinking results in cancellation of the Children's Overseas Reception Board's plan to relocate British children abroad.

September

23rd   King George VI announces the creation of the George Cross decoration during a radio broadcast.

27th   The Battle of Graveney Marsh in Kent, the last exchange of shots with a foreign force on mainland British soil, takes place when soldiers of the London Irish Rifles capture the crew of a downed new German Junkers Ju 88 bomber who initially resist arrest with gunfire; one of the enemies is shot in the foot.

October

9th   Winston Churchill succeeds Neville Chamberlain as Leader of the Conservative Party.

14th   At least 64 people are killed when a German bomb penetrates Balham station on the London Underground which is in use as an air-raid shelter.

25th   Air Chief Marshal Sir Charles Portal is appointed to succeed Sir Cyril Newall as Chief of the Air Staff, a post he will hold for the remainder of the War.

31st   The Battle of Britain ends.

November

6th   Fourteen children are killed when a German bomb hits the Civic Centre in Southampton.

November

11th	Battle of Taranto: the Royal Navy launches the first aircraft carrier strike in history, on the Italian fleet at Taranto.
14th	Coventry Blitz: the centre of Coventry is destroyed by 500 German Luftwaffe bombers: 150,000 incendiary devices, 503 tons of high explosives and 130 parachute mines level 60,000 of the city's 75,000 buildings. At least 568 people are killed, while 863 more are injured. Exceptionally, the location and nature of the damage here is immediately publicised in the media. Below is what is left of the Cathedral in Coventry.

19th	Less than a week after the blitz of Coventry, further heavy air raids take place in central England. Birmingham, West Bromwich, Dudley and Tipton are all bombed. Some 900 people are killed and 2,000 more injured – there are 53 deaths at the Birmingham Small Arms Company factory in Small Heath alone. Most of the region's casualties are in Birmingham.

November

24th | The Bristol Blitz was the heavy bombing of Bristol, England by the Nazi German Luftwaffe during the Second World War. Due to the presence of Bristol Harbour and the Bristol Aeroplane Company the city was a target for bombing, and was easily found as enemy bombers were able to trace a course up the River Avon from Avonmouth using reflected moonlight on the waters into the heart of the city. Bristol was the fifth most heavily bombed British city of World War II.

December

12th | The Sheffield Blitz is the name given to the worst nights of German Luftwaffe bombing in Sheffield, England, during the Second World War. It took place over the nights of 12th December and the 15th December 1940. In 1940 Sheffield was a city of about 560,000 people and contained many heavy industries, primarily centred on steel and armaments. Hadfield's steelworks was also the only place in the UK at that time where 18-inch armour-piercing shells were made. Most of the factories were located in the East end of the city beside the River Don. Documents captured at the end of the war showed that the targets for the raids included the Atlas Steelworks, Brown Bayley Steelworks, Meadowhall Iron Works, River Don Works, Darnall Wagon Works, Tinsley Park Collieries, East Hecla Works and Orgreave Coke Ovens. The full moon was on the 14th December 1940 and both blitz nights were cold and clear.

14th | Release of the Ealing Studios war comedy Sailors Three, starring Tommy Trinder, Claude Hulbert and Michael Wilding; the song "All Over The Place", sung by Trinder in the film (words by Frank Eyton; music by Noel Gay), becomes one of the most popular of the war.

20th | An anti-aircraft shell fired from Dudley accidentally strikes a public house in neighbouring Tipton, resulting in dozens of casualties.

21st | Liverpool Blitz: Liverpool is heavily bombed, with well over 300 people killed and hundreds more injured.

22nd | Manchester Blitz: Manchester is heavily bombed as the Luftwaffe air raids on Britain continue. 363 are killed and 1,183 wounded; and Manchester Cathedral is badly damaged.

29th | Heavy bombing in London causes the Second Great Fire of London. Guildhall is among many buildings badly damaged or destroyed. There are hundreds more casualties.

Whatever the pleasure
Player's complete it

PLAYER'S NAVY CUT CIGARETTES & TOBACCO

Issued by The Imperial Tobacco Company (of Great Britain and Ireland), Ltd.   [NCC.804]

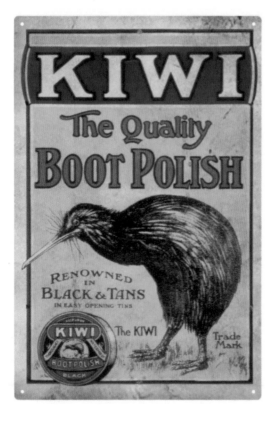

until I see you again dearest — your sweet face is always in my heart and I can almost feel your soft smooth cheek against mine.
Love — Jim

Just for him —

GUARD YOUR LOVELINESS!
USE THE ONE LEADING BEAUTY SOAP...
MADE WITH OLIVE AND PALM OILS!

WHEN HE COMES HOME, will he find you as lovely as his heart has dreamed you'd be? Day's end or year's end...will the sweet look, the soft touch of you...be just as he remembered?

For his sake, guard your loveliness. Choose your beauty soap with care and caution. *Know* what it is made with!

Consider, for example, that of all leading soaps, Palmolive *alone* is made with Olive and Palm Oils. Into its making go no animal fats...only those fine vegetable oils...treasured as beauty aids since Cleopatra's day.

No wonder millions of women thrill to the way Palmolive helps keep skin smooth, petal-soft and at its radiant best. No wonder Palmolive is the world's largest-selling beauty soap. To guard the loveliness *he* loves...turn *now* to Palmolive's gentle care!

Remember
PALMOLIVE'S BEAUTY OILS...

olive and palm oils — no others — go into the making of Palmolive. Look for the olive color.

PALMOLIVE

NOW MORE THAN EVER...KEEP THAT SCHOOLGIRL COMPLEXION

HOW THE FISHERS FACED THE BOMBERS REVEALING INTERVIEWS | RACING AND FOOTBALL POOL SHOTS COMPLETE LIST OF ALL EVENTS

TOPICAL TIMES

NO. 1052. [REGISTERED AS A NEWSPAPER AT G.P.O.] WEEK ENDING JANUARY 13, 1940. PRICE 2D.

The Gift of being well-groomed

BRYLCREEM

THE PERFECT HAIR DRESSING

TONIGHT they're dining at the Mayfair; then on to a theatre and dancing till the early hours. Tomorrow they're full up too —not an evening before Friday week. You see them everywhere, the man-about-town and his constant companion—Brylcreem. However long the night, Brylcreem keeps his hair immaculate. Christmas is a busy time for them both, and he can always do with an extra jar. The big bottle with the pump attachment makes an ideal gift.

In bottles and tubes **1/-**

Larger bottles **1/6 1/9 2/6**

Pumps to fit bottles . . . 2/-

At all Chemists and Hairdressers

COST OF LIVING 1940

A conversion of pre-decimal to decimal money

The Pound, 1971 became the year of decimalization when the pound became 100 new pennies. Prior to that the pound was equivalent to 20 shillings. Money prior to 1971 was written £/s/d. (d being for pence). Below is a chart explaining the monetary value of each coin before and after 1971.

Symbol	Before 1971	After 1971
£	**Pound (240 pennies)**	**Pound (100 new pennies)**
s	Shilling (12 pennies)	5 pence
d	**Penny**	**¼ of a penny**
¼d	Farthing	1 penny
½d	**Halfpenny**	**½ pence**
3d	Threepence	About 1/80 of a pound
4d	**Groat (four pennies)**	
6d	Sixpence (Tanner)	2½ new pence
2s	**Florin (2 shillings)**	**10 pence**
2s/6d	Half a crown (2 shillings and 6 pence)	12½ pence
5s	**Crown**	**25 pence**
10s	10 shilling note (10 bob)	50 pence
10s/6d	**½ Guinea**	**52½ pence**
21s	1 Guinea	105 pence

Prices are in equivalent to new pence today and on average throughout the UK.

Item	1940	Price equivalent today
Wages, average yearly	**£185.00**	**£10,905.00**
Average house price	£530.00	£31,217.00
Price of an average car	**£310.00**	**£18,259.00**
Litre of petrol	£0.02p	£1.30p
Flour 1.5kg	**£0.03p**	**£1.53p**
Bread (loaf)	£0.02p	£0.94p
Sugar 1kg	**£0.04p**	**£2.53p**
Milk 1 pint	£0.06p	£3.53p
Butter 250g	**£0.04p**	**£2.53p**
Cheese 400g	£0.05p	£2.85p
Potatoes 2.5kg	**£0.03p**	**£1.62p**
Bacon 400g	£0.11p	£6.60p
Beer (Pint)	**£0.05p**	**£3.67p**

How much did things cost in 1940?

Rowntree's Cocoa, 6d (2½p) per ¼lb.

Chappie Dog Food, 7d (3p) per tin.
Black Cat cigarettes, 10 for 6d (2½p).

Reckitt's Bath Cubes, 2d (1p) each.
A small bungalow, £250.
10 hp Vauxhall saloon car, £169.

Drene Shampoo, 6d (2½p), 1/- (5p) and 2/6 (12½p) per bottle.

Maltesers, 2d (1p) per packet, 6d (2½p) per box.
Oxydol, sold in 3½d (1½p), 6d (2½p) and 1/- (5p) pkts.

Wrigley's PK Chewing Gum, 1d (½p) per packet.

Halls Wine, 3/9 (19p) and 6/6 (32½p) per bottle.
Celanese ties, cost 1/6 (7½p) each.

The Scottish Motor Traction Co Ltd advised that the fare from Glasgow to London was £1/10/- (£1.50p) and the return fare was £2/10/- (£2.50p).

120 Wills 'Gold Flake' cigarettes could be sent to the British Forces in France for 3/9 (18½p).

Seats in London's 'His Majesty's Theatre' to see Stanley Lupino, Florence Desmond & Sally Gray in 'Funny Side Up' cost from 1/6 to 10/6 (7½p to 52½p).

CALENDAR OF 1940

1940

January

	Sun	Mon	Tue	Wed	Thu	Fri	Sat
2		1	2	3	4	5	6
3	7	8	9	10	11	12	13
4	14	15	16	17	18	19	20
5	21	22	23	24	25	26	27
6	28	29	30	31			

February

	Sun	Mon	Tue	Wed	Thu	Fri	Sat
6					1	2	3
7	4	5	6	7	8	9	10
8	11	12	13	14	15	16	17
9	18	19	20	21	22	23	24
10	25	26	27	28	29		

March

	Sun	Mon	Tue	Wed	Thu	Fri	Sat
10						1	2
11	3	4	5	6	7	8	9
12	10	11	12	13	14	15	16
13	17	18	19	20	21	22	23
14	24	25	26	27	28	29	30
15	31						

April

	Sun	Mon	Tue	Wed	Thu	Fri	Sat
15		1	2	3	4	5	6
16	7	8	9	10	11	12	13
17	14	15	16	17	18	19	20
18	21	22	23	24	25	26	27
19	28	29	30				

May

	Sun	Mon	Tue	Wed	Thu	Fri	Sat
19				1	2	3	4
20	5	6	7	8	9	10	11
21	12	13	14	15	16	17	18
22	19	20	21	22	23	24	25
23	26	27	28	29	30	31	

June

	Sun	Mon	Tue	Wed	Thu	Fri	Sat
23							1
24	2	3	4	5	6	7	8
25	9	10	11	12	13	14	15
26	16	17	18	19	20	21	22
27	23	24	25	26	27	28	29
28	30						

July

	Sun	Mon	Tue	Wed	Thu	Fri	Sat
28		1	2	3	4	5	6
29	7	8	9	10	11	12	13
30	14	15	16	17	18	19	20
31	21	22	23	24	25	26	27
32	28	29	30	31			

August

	Sun	Mon	Tue	Wed	Thu	Fri	Sat
32				1	2	3	
33	4	5	6	7	8	9	10
34	11	12	13	14	15	16	17
35	18	19	20	21	22	23	24
36	25	26	27	28	29	30	31

Setptember

	Sun	Mon	Tue	Wed	Thu	Fri	Sat
37	1	2	3	4	5	6	7
38	8	9	10	11	12	13	14
39	15	16	17	18	19	20	21
40	22	23	24	25	26	27	28
41	29	30					

October

	Sun	Mon	Tue	Wed	Thu	Fri	Sat
41		1	2	3	4	5	
42	6	7	8	9	10	11	12
43	13	14	15	16	17	18	19
44	20	21	22	23	24	25	26
45	27	28	29	30	31		

November

	Sun	Mon	Tue	Wed	Thu	Fri	Sat
45						1	2
46	3	4	5	6	7	8	9
47	10	11	12	13	14	15	16
48	17	18	19	20	21	22	23
49	24	25	26	27	28	29	30

December

	Sun	Mon	Tue	Wed	Thu	Fri	Sat
50	1	2	3	4	5	6	7
51	8	9	10	11	12	13	14
52	15	16	17	18	19	20	21
53	22	23	24	25	26	27	28
54	29	30	31				

BRITISH BIRTHS

Michael Reid was born on the 19th January 1940 and born in Hackney, London. Michael sadly passed away on the 29th July 2007. He was an English comedian, actor, author and occasional television presenter from London who is best remembered for playing the role of Frank Butcher in EastEnders and hosting the popular children's TV show Runaround. He started his career as comedian doing the pub circuit and then became one of the original stars of The Comedians, a popular TV series of the 1970s. He capitalised on his initial success with a one-off hit record, a novelty version of The Ugly Duckling recorded on Pye records. In 1975 it reached number 10 in the BBC singles chart. In 1987, he joined the cast of popular BBC television soap opera EastEnders as Frank Butcher, for which he gained much popularity over the years. He initially joined the series as a semi-regular character, first appearing in September of that year, but was so popular that during 1988 he became a full-time cast member as his character became landlord of the Queen Vic pub.

Sir John Vincent Hurt CBE was born on the 22nd January 1940 and passed away on the 25th January 2017. He was born in Chesterfield, Derbyshire and was an English actor whose career spanned more than 50 years. John Hurt's first film was The Wild and the Willing (1962), but his first major role was as Richard Rich in A Man for All Seasons (1966). He played Timothy Evans, who was hanged for murders committed by his landlord John Christie, in 10 Rillington Place (1971), earning him his first BAFTA nomination for Best Supporting Actor. His portrayal of Quentin Crisp in the TV play The Naked Civil Servant (1975) gave him prominence and earned him the British Academy Television Award for Best Actor. In the first Harry Potter film, Harry Potter and the Philosopher's Stone (2001), he played Mr Ollivander, the wand-maker. He returned for the adaptation of Harry Potter and the Goblet of Fire, though his scenes in that film were cut. He also returned for Harry Potter and the Deathly Hallows – Part 1 and Part 2.

Sir David John White, OBE was born on the 2nd February 1940 known professionally as by his stage name David Jason. He was born in Edmonton, Middlesex and English actor, comedian, screenwriter and television producer. He is best known for his roles as Derek "Del Boy" Trotter in the BBC comedy series sitcom Only Fools and Horses, Detective Inspector Jack Frost in A Touch of Frost, Granville in Open All Hours and Still Open All Hours, and Pop Larkin in The Darling Buds of May, as well as voicing Mr. Toad in The Wind in the Willows and the title characters of Danger Mouse and Count Duckula. His last original appearance as Del Boy was in 2014, while Jason retired his role as Frost in 2010. In September 2006 Jason topped the poll to find TV's 50 Greatest Stars, as part of ITV's 50th anniversary celebrations. He was knighted in 2005 for services to drama. Jason has won four British Academy Television Awards (BAFTAs), (1988, 1991, 1997, 2003), four British Comedy Awards (1990, 1992, 1997, 2001) and seven National Television Awards (1996 twice, 1997, 2001 twice, 2002 and 2011).

James Joseph Tarbuck OBE was born on the 6th February 1940 and grew up in Wavertree, Liverpool and is an English comedian. His first television show was Its Tarbuck '65! on ITV in 1964, though he had been introduced at the London Palladium on 27 October 1963 by Bruce Forsyth. In the 1980s he hosted similar Sunday night variety shows, Live From Her Majesty's, Live from the Piccadilly and finally Live from the Palladium.

Jimmy Tarbuck made a Comedy Playhouse pilot for the BBC in 1967, acting in Johnny Speight's To Lucifer, A Son alongside John Le Mesurier and Pat Coombs, but a series was not commissioned.

In October 2015, Tarbuck and Des O'Connor starred in their own one-off show at the London Palladium to raise money for the new Royal Variety Charity. During the following two years they toured clubs and theatres around the UK with his comedy show, and sometimes as a double act with Kenny Lynch.

James Peter Greaves was born on the 20th February 1940 and was born in Manor Park, England. He is a former England international footballer who played as a forward. He is England's fourth highest international goal scorer with 44 goals, Tottenham Hotspur's highest ever goal scorer with 266 goals, the highest goal scorer in the history of English top-flight football with 357 goals, and has also scored more hat-tricks (six) for England than anyone else. Jimmy began his professional career at Chelsea in 1957, and played in the following year's FA Youth Cup final. He scored 124 First Division goals in just four seasons before being sold on to Italian club A.C. Milan for £80,000 in April 1961 Whilst with Spurs he won the FA Cup in 1961–62 and 1966–67, the Charity Shield in 1962 and 1967, and the European Cup Winners' Cup in 1962–63; he never won a league title but did help Spurs to a second-place finish in 1962–63. After retiring as a player Greaves went on to enjoy a successful career in broadcasting, most notably working alongside Ian St John on Saint and Greavsie from 1985 to 1992.

David McPherson Broome CBE was born on the 1st March 1940 and is a retired Welsh show jumping champion. He competed in the 1960, 1964, 1968, 1972 and 1988 Olympics and won individual bronze medals in 1960 and 1968 on his best-known horse Mr Softee. In 1960, he was also voted BBC Sports Personality of the Year, and at the 1972 Games served as the Olympic flag bearer for Great Britain. David was born in Cardiff, attended Monmouth School, and still maintains his stables at Mount Ballan Manor, Crick, near Chepstow in Monmouthshire. He held the individual European title in 1961, 1967 and 1969. In 1970, he won the world title and became Western Mail Welsh Sports Personality of the year. He turned professional in 1973, and in 1978 helped the British team to win the world championship. Broome has won the King George V Gold Cup a record six times on six different horses between 1960–1991, a record yet to be equalled. He has enjoyed most of his success on Irish Sport Horses and he has said his favourite horse of all was Sportsman.

Annie Avril Nightingale, MBE was born on the 1st April 1940 is an English radio and television broadcaster. She was born in Osterley, London and was the first female presenter on BBC Radio 1 and is its longest-serving presenter. Her first broadcast on the BBC was on the 14th September 1963 as a panellist on Juke Box Jury, and she contributed to Woman's Hour in 1964 and hosted programmes on the BBC Light Programme in 1966.

She started at Radio 1 on the 8th February 1970 with a Sunday evening show. The show is short lived and in April she became one of the hosts of the singles review show What's New before graduating to a late-night progressive rock show, which was simulcast on the BBC Radio 2's FM frequency. In 1978, Nightingale became the main presenter of The Old Grey Whistle Test on BBC2 as a replacement for long-time host Bob Harris. In 1994, Nightingale moved to a weekend overnight dance music show initially called The Chill Out Zone. She can still be heard in the early hours of Wednesday mornings on BBC Radio 1 and 1Xtra.

Dame Penelope Anne Constance Keith, DBE, DL was born on the 2nd April 1940 and grew up in Sutton, Surrey. She is an English actress including radio, stage, television and film and primarily known for her roles in the British sitcoms The Good Life and To the Manor Born. Penelope Keith joined the Royal Shakespeare Company in 1963, and went on to win the 1976 Olivier Award for Best Comedy Performance for the play Donkeys' Years. She became a household name in the UK playing Margo Leadbetter in the sitcom The Good Life (1975–78), winning the 1977 BAFTA TV Award for Best Light Entertainment Performance. In 2004, Penelope Keith starred in the first of 5 full-cast BBC radio dramatizations of M.C. Beaton's Agatha Raisin novels, playing the title role. Two years later, she appeared at the Chichester Festival in the premiere of Richard Everett's comedy Entertaining Angels, which she later took on tour. In early 2018, she presented the Channel 4 series Village of the Year with Penelope Keith.

Jeffrey Howard Archer was born on the 15th April 1940 and raised up in Finsbury, London. He is an English novelist, former politician, and peer of the realm. Jeffery Archer became deputy chairman of the Conservative Party (1985–86), before resigning after a newspaper accused him of paying money to a prostitute. In 1987, he won a court case and was awarded large damages because of this claim. He was made a life peer in 1992 and subsequently became Conservative candidate to be the first elected Mayor of London. He had to resign his candidacy in 1999 after it emerged that he had lied in his 1987 libel case. He was imprisoned (2001–03) for perjury and perverting the course of justice, ending his elected political career. Archer wrote his first book, Not a Penny More, Not a Penny Less, in the autumn of 1974, as a means of avoiding bankruptcy. The book was picked up by the literary agent Deborah Owen and published first in the U.S., then eventually in Britain in the autumn of 1976. A radio adaptation was aired on BBC Radio 4 in the early 1980s and a BBC Television adaptation of the book was broadcast in 1990.

Ronald Wycherley better known by his stage name Billy Fury. He was born on the 17th April 1940 and passed away on the 28th January 1983. He was an English singer from the late 1950s to the mid-1960s, and remained an active songwriter until the 1980s. He was born in Liverpool, Lancashire. As an early British rock and roll (and film) star, he equalled the Beatles' record of 24 hits in the 1960s, and spent 332 weeks on the UK chart, without a chart-topping single or album. He released his first hit single for Decca, "Maybe Tomorrow", in 1959. He also appeared in a televised play Strictly for Sparrows, and subsequently on Oh Boy! In March 1960, he reached No. 9 in the UK Singles Chart with his own composition "Colette", followed by "That's Love" and his first album The Sound of Fury (1960), which featured a young Joe Brown on lead guitar, with backup vocals by the Four Jays. Having had more UK hits, such as "It's Only Make Believe" and "I Will", both in 1964, and "In Thoughts of You" (1965), Fury began a lengthy absence from the charts in 1967, and underwent surgery for heart problems in 1972 and 1976 which led to him abandoning his tours.

Sir Thomas John Woodward OBE was born on the 7th June 1940 and is known professionally as Tom Jones. Tom was born and raised in Treforest, Pontypridd, Glamorgan, Wales. Tom Jones manager finally got a recording contract with Decca. His first single, "Chills and Fever", was released in late 1964. It did not chart, but the follow-up, "its Not Unusual", became an international hit after offshore pirate radio station Radio Caroline promoted it. The following year was the most prominent of Jones's career, making him one of the most popular vocalists of the British Invasion. In early 1965, "its Not Unusual" reached No. 1 in the United Kingdom and the top ten in the United States. During 1965, Mills secured a number of film themes for Jones to record, including the theme songs for the film What's New Pussycat? And also for the James Bond film Thunderball. Tom was also awarded the Grammy Award for Best New Artist in 1966. In 1987, Tom Jones re-entered the singles chart with "A Boy From Nowhere", which went to No. 2 in the UK. Tom Jones and his idol Elvis Presley met in 1965 at the Paramount film stage, when Elvis was filming Paradise, Hawaiian Style. They became good friends until Elvis passed away in 1977.

Terence Nelhams-Wright was born on the 23rd June 1940 and passed away on the 8th March 2003. He was well known as Adam Faith, was an English teen idol, singer, actor and financial journalist. He was one of the most charted acts of the 1960s. He became the first UK artist to lodge his initial seven hits in the Top 5. He was also one of the first UK acts to record original songs regularly. Adam Faith began his musical career in 1957, while working as a film cutter in London in the hope of becoming an actor, singing with and managing a skiffle group, the Worried Men. Faith's success on Drumbeat enabled another recording contract, with Parlophone. His next record in 1959, "What Do You Want?", written by Les Vandyke and produced by Barry and John Burgess, received good reviews in the NME and other papers, as well as being voted a hit on Juke Box Jury. This became his first number one hit in the UK Singles Chart, and his pronunciation of the word 'baby' as 'bay-beh' became a catchphrase. With his next two single releases, "Poor Me" and "Someone Else's Baby", Faith established himself as a prominent rival to Cliff Richard in British popular music.

Sir Richard Starkey MBE was born on the 7th July 1940 who is better known professionally as Ringo Starr. He was born in Dingle, Liverpool and is an English musician, singer, songwriter and actor who gained worldwide fame as the drummer for the Beatles. In 1957, he co-founded his first band, the Eddie Clayton Skiffle Group, which earned several prestigious local bookings before the fad succumbed to American rock and roll by early 1958. When the Beatles formed in 1960, Starr was a member of another Liverpool group, Rory Storm and the Hurricanes. After achieving moderate success in the UK and Hamburg, he quit the Hurricanes and joined the Beatles in August 1962, replacing Pete Best. After the band's break-up in 1970, he released several successful singles including the US number-four hit "It Don't Come Easy", and number ones "Photograph" and "You're Sixteen". In 1972, he released his most successful UK single, "Back Off Boogaloo", which peaked at number two. He is the richest drummer in the world with a net worth of US$350 million.

Sir Patrick Stewart OBE was born on the 13th July 1940 and grew up in Mirfield, Yorkshire and is an English actor whose work has included roles on stage, television, and film in a career spanning almost six decades. In January 1967, he made his debut TV appearance on Coronation Street as a fire officer. In 1969, he had a brief TV cameo role as Horatio, opposite Ian Richardson's Hamlet, in a performance of the gravedigger scene as part of episode six of Sir Kenneth Clark's Civilisation television series. When Stewart was picked for the role of Captain Jean-Luc Picard in Star Trek: The Next Generation (1987–94), the Los Angeles Times called him an "unknown British Shakespearean actor". Still living out of his suitcase because of his scepticism that the show would succeed. From 1994 to 2002, he also portrayed Picard in the film's Star Trek Generations (1994), Star Trek: First Contact (1996), Star Trek: Insurrection (1998) and Star Trek: Nemesis (2002); and in Star Trek: Deep Space Nine's pilot episode "Emissary", and received a 1995 Screen Actors Guild Award nomination for "Outstanding Performance by a Male Actor in a Drama Series".

Timothy Julian Brooke-Taylor OBE was born on the 17th July 1940 and was born in Buxton, Derbyshire. He is an English comedian and actor and became active in performing in comedy sketches while at Cambridge University, and became President of the Footlights club, touring internationally with the Footlights revue in 1964.

Becoming wider known to the public for his work on BBC Radio with I'm Sorry, I'll Read That Again, he moved into television with At Last the 1948 Show working together with old Cambridge friends John Cleese and Graham Chapman. He is most well known as a member of The Goodies, starring in the television series throughout the 1970s and picking up international recognition in Australia and New Zealand. He has also appeared as an actor in various sitcoms, and has been a panellist on I'm Sorry I Haven't a Clue for over 40 years.

John Winston Ono Lennon MBE was born on the 9th October 1940 and died on the 8th December 1980. He was an English singer, songwriter and peace activist who gained worldwide fame as the founder, co-lead vocalist, and rhythm guitarist of the Beatles. His song writing partnership with Paul McCartney remains the most successful in history. Born in Liverpool, John Lennon became involved in the skiffle craze as a teenager. In 1957, he formed his first band, the Quarrymen, which evolved into the Beatles in 1960. After moving to New York City in 1971, his criticism of the Vietnam War resulted in a three-year attempt by the Nixon administration to deport him. In 1975, Lennon disengaged from the music business to raise his infant son Sean, and in 1980, returned with the Ono collaboration Double Fantasy. He was shot and killed in the archway of his Manhattan apartment building three weeks after the album's release. By 2012, Lennon's solo album sales in the US had exceeded 14 million units. He had 25 number-one singles on the US Billboard chart as a writer, co-writer or performer.

Sir Cliff Richard OBE born Harry Rodger Webb on the 14th October 1940 is a British singer, musician, performer, actor and philanthropist. Cliff Richard has sold more than 250 million records worldwide. He has total sales of over 21 million singles in the United Kingdom and is the third-top-selling artist in UK Singles Chart history, behind the Beatles and Elvis Presley. Over a career spanning 60 years, Richard has amassed many gold and platinum discs and awards, including two Ivor Novello Awards and three Brit Awards. More than 130 of his singles, albums and EPs have reached the UK Top 20, more than any other artist. Cliff Richard has been a resident in the United Kingdom for most of his life, though in 2010, he confirmed that he had become a citizen of Barbados. Cliff Richard's 1958 hit "Move It" is widely regarded as the first authentic British rock and roll record, and "laid the foundations" for the Beatles and Merseybeat music. John Lennon said of Cliff Richard: "before Cliff and the Shadows, there had been nothing worth listening to in British music".

Sir Michael John Gambon CBE was born on the 19th October 1940 and is an Irish-born British character actor who has worked in theatre, television, and film. He is also known as The Great Gambon as dubbed by actor Ralph Richardson. He was trained under Laurence Olivier and started his long work on stage in the National Theatre. He received a Tony Award nomination for Best Actor in a Play for his work in David Hare's Skylight on Broadway. Gambon retired from stage acting in 2015 due to memory loss. Michael Gambon is most famous for portraying Professor Albus Dumbledore in the final six Harry Potter films after the death of Richard Harris who had previously played the role. His other films include, The Cook, the Thief, His Wife & Her Lover (1989), The Wings of the Dove (1997), Amazing Grace (2006), The King's Speech (2010), and Quartet (2012). Gambon has appeared in various television projects including, The Singing Detective (1986), Wives and Daughters (1999), Path to War (2002), Cranford (2007), Emma (2009), The Casual Vacancy (2015), Churchill's Secret (2016), The Hollow Crown (2016), and Little Women (2017).

SPORTING EVENTS 1940

British Formula 1 Grand Prix

Naturally, the war put paid to international motor racing, although the Tripoli Grand Prix was held in 1940, and won by Farina's Alfa Romeo at 128.22 mph from the Alfas of Biondetti and the veteran Count Trossi. It was to be some years before racing found its feet again, however. Wars may disrupt and eventually quell motor racing but they have never spelt the end of its continuity. So it was in 1914-18 and again in 1939-1945.

World War 2 may have changed the whole way of European life as had the conflict of a quarter of a century earlier and it certainly left Europe in a shattered condition: her motor car manufacturing plants were either destroyed or converted for the production of aircraft and munitions. All through the dark years of this tremendous struggle for power, with bombs raining down on towns and factories, the enthusiasm for motor competitions never wained

Brooklands had been severely damaged by the onset of World War II and the circuit was abandoned. Most new British circuits were being built on disused Royal Air Force airfields, and Silverstone, located in Northamptonshire in central England, was one of those circuits. It staged its first race, the Royal Automobile Club International Grand Prix on 2 October 1948, which was won by Italian Luigi Villoresi in a Maserati. In 1949, the circuit was heavily modified and made very fast; and it remained in this configuration for decades on.

1940 County Cricket Season

All first-class cricket was cancelled in the 1940 to 1944 English cricket seasons because of the Second World War; no first-class matches were played in England after Friday, 1st September 1939 until Saturday, 19th May 1945.

Ten matches were cancelled at the end of the 1939 English cricket season due to the German invasion of Poland on 1st September and the British government's declaration of war against Germany on Sunday 3rd September.

Although eleven first-class matches were arranged during the 1945 season following the final defeat of Germany in early May, it was not until the 1946 season that normal fixtures, including the County Championship and Minor Counties Championship, could resume. In contrast with much of the First World War, it was realised in the 1940s that cricket had its part to play in terms of raising both public morale and funds for charity. Efforts were made to stage matches whenever opportunity arose, especially if a suitable number of top players could be assembled. From the summer of 1941 onwards, teams such as the British Empire Eleven toured the country raising money for war charities.

At league cricket level, playing one-day matches, many competitions continued throughout the war: e.g., the Birmingham League, the Bradford League and the Lancashire League.

One venue where it would not be possible was The Oval, which was commandeered in 1939 and quickly turned into a prisoner of war camp, except that no prisoners were ever interned there. The playing area became a maze of concrete posts and wire fences.

Lord's was also due for requisition but it was spared and MCC was able to stage many public schools and representative games throughout the war. A highlight in 1940 was the one-day game in which Sir PF Warner's XI, including Len Hutton and Denis Compton (who top-scored with 73), beat a West Indies XI which included Learie Constantine and Leslie Compton (an honorary West Indian for the day).

Of the more regular wartime teams, the most famous were the British Empire XI and the London Counties XI which were established in 1940. Both played one-day charity matches, mostly in the south-east and often at Lord's. The British Empire XI was founded by Pelham Warner but featured mainly English county players. The politician Desmond Donnelly, then in the Royal Air Force, began the London Counties XI. In one match between the two, Frank Woolley came out of retirement and played against the new star batsman Denis Compton. The British Empire XI played between 34 and 45 matches per season from 1940 to 1944; the London Counties XI was credited with 191 matches from 1940 to 1945.

Although the teams were successful in raising money for charity, their main purpose was to help sustain morale. Many of the services and civil defence organisations had their own teams, some of them national and featuring first-class players.

County clubs encouraged their players to join the services but at the same time pleaded with their members to continue subscriptions "as an investment for the future". While some counties (notably Somerset and Hampshire) closed for the duration, others did arrange matches. Nottinghamshire played six matches at Trent Bridge in 1940 and Lancashire mooted a scheme for a regionalised county competition to include the minor counties, but it was not taken further.

The Masters 1940

The 1940 Masters Tournament was the seventh Masters Tournament, held April 4–7 at Augusta National Golf Club in Augusta, Georgia.

Jimmy Demaret won the first of his three Masters titles, four strokes ahead of runner-up Lloyd Mangrum, the largest margin of victory until 1948. The purse was $5,000 and the winner's share was $1,500.

Mangrum shot an opening round 64 (−8), a new course record by two strokes, and it stood for 46 years, until Nick Price's 63 in 1986, later equalled by Greg Norman in 1996. Although all three of these players won major titles, none won a Masters.

Place	Player	Country	Score	To par	Money ($)
1	Jimmy Demaret	United States	67-72-70-71=280	−8	1,500
2	Lloyd Mangrum	United States	64-75-71-74=284	−4	800
3	Byron Nelson	United States	69-72-74-70=285	−3	600
T4	Harry Cooper	England United States	69-75-73-70=287	−1	400
T4	Ed Dudley	United States	73-72-71-71=287	−1	400
T4	Willie Goggin	United States	71-72-73-71=287	−1	400
T7	Henry Picard	United States	71-71-71-75=288	E	200
T7	Sam Snead	United States	71-72-69-76=288	E	200
T7	Craig Wood	United States	70-75-67-76=288	E	200
T10	Ben Hogan	United States	73-74-69-74=290	+2	100
T10	Toney Penna	Italy United States	73-73-72-72=290	+2	100

Augusta National Golf Club, sometimes referred to as Augusta or the National, is one of the most famous and exclusive golf clubs in the world, located in Augusta, Georgia, United States. Unlike most private clubs which operate as non-profits, Augusta National is a for-profit corporation, and it does not disclose its income, holdings, membership list, or ticket sales.

Founded by Bobby Jones and Clifford Roberts, the course was designed by Jones and Alister MacKenzie and opened for play in 1932. Since 1934, the club has played host to the annual Masters Tournament, one of the four major championships in professional golf, and the only major played each year at the same course. It was the top-ranked course in Golf Digest's 2009 list of America's 100 greatest courses and was the number ten-ranked course based on course architecture on Golfweek Magazine's 2011 list of best classic courses in the United States.

1940 Grand National

The 1940 Grand National was the 99th renewal of the world-famous Grand National horse race that took place at Aintree Racecourse near Liverpool, England, on the 5th April 1940.

Thirty horses ran in the steeplechase, which was won by Bogskar, a 25/1 shot ridden by Royal Air Force sergeant Mervyn Jones. MacMoffat finished in second place, Gold Arrow was third and Symaethis fourth.

It was the last true Aintree Grand National before a five-year break due to World War II.

Position	Name	Jockey	Age	Handicap (st-lb)	SP	Distance
01	Bogskar	Mervyn Jones	7	10-4	25/1	4 lengths
02	MacMoffat	Ian Alder	8	10-10		
03	Gold Arrow	Peter Lay	8	10-3		
04	Symaethis	Matthew Feakes	8	10-7		

Horse racing flat winners of 1940

Event	Horse	Jockey	Trainer
1000 Guineas	**Godiva**	**Doug Marks**	**William Jarvis**
2000 Guineas	Djebel	Charlie Elliot	Albert Swann
The Derby	**Pont L'Eveque**	**Sam Wragg**	**Fred Darling**
The Oaks	Godiva	Doug Marks	William Jarvis
St Ledger Stakes	**Turkhan**	**Gordon Richards**	**Frank Butters**

Godiva (1937–1940) was a British Thoroughbred racehorse, best known for winning two Classics in 1940. The filly won six times from eight races in a racing career which lasted from 1939 until June 1940. After winning three times as a two-year-old she was unbeaten in 1940, winning the 1000 Guineas over one mile at Newmarket and a wartime substitute Oaks over one and a half miles at the same course a month later. Godiva died within five months of her final race. She has been described as one of the best British race mares of the 20th century.

BOOKS PUBLISHED IN 1940

Sad Cypress is a work of detective fiction by British writer Agatha Christie, first published in the UK by the Collins Crime Club in March 1940 and in the US by Dodd, Mead and Company later in the same year. Elinor Carlisle and Roddy Welman are engaged to be married when she receives an anonymous letter claiming that someone is "sucking up" to their wealthy aunt, Laura Welman, from whom Elinor and Roddy expect to inherit a sizeable fortune. Elinor suspects Mary Gerrard as the topic of the anonymous letter, the lodge keeper's daughter, whom their aunt likes and supports. Neither guesses who wrote the letter, which is burned.

Mrs Welman is partially paralyzed after a stroke and dislikes living that way. She tells both her physician Peter Lord and her niece how much she dislikes living without full health, wishing the doctor might end her pain, which he refuses to do. Roddy falls in love with Mary; this provokes Elinor to end their engagement. After a second stroke, Mrs Welman asks Elinor to make provision for Mary. Elinor assumes there is a will her aunt wants modified. Mrs Welman dies before Elinor can call the solicitor. There is no will. She dies intestate, so her considerable estate goes to Elinor outright as her only known surviving blood relative.

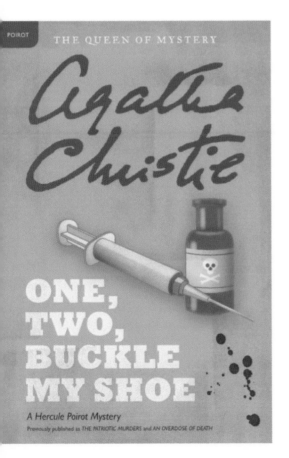

One, Two, Buckle My Shoe is a work of detective fiction by Agatha Christie first published in the United Kingdom by the Collins Crime Club in November 1940.

Hercule Poirot meets former actress Mabelle Sainsbury Seale while leaving his appointment with dentist Henry Morley. In this meeting, he helps retrieves a shiny buckle for her that had fallen from her shoe. Later that day, his friend Inspector Japp informs him that Morley has been found dead, having been shot in the head. Between Poirot's appointment and Morley's death, the dentist had three patients - along with Mabelle, he also dealt with Alistair Blunt, a prominent banker, and a Greek spy known only as Amberiotis. A fourth person was present at the surgery, Howard Raikes, an American left-wing activist who disliked Blunt but is enamoured with his niece, Jane Olivera. Amberiotis is later found dead from an overdose of anaesthetic, leading to the belief that Morley accidentally killed him and committed suicide upon realizing his mistake. Poirot disagrees with this belief. He learns that prior to Morley's death, his secretary Gladys Nevill had been called away by a fake telegram and that her boyfriend Frank Carter was disliked by the dentist.

Four Quartets is a set of four poems written by T. S. Eliot that were published over a six-year period. The first poem, Burnt Norton, was published with a collection of his early works (1936's Collected Poems 1909–1935.) After a few years, Eliot composed the other three poems, East Coker, The Dry Salvages, and Little Gidding, which were written during World War II and the air-raids on Great Britain. They were first published as a series by Faber and Faber in Great Britain between 1940 and 1942 towards the end of Eliot's poetic career (East Coker in September 1940, Burnt Norton in February 1941, The Dry Salvages in September 1941 and Little Gidding in 1942.) The poems were not collected until Eliot's New York publisher printed them together in 1943.

Four Quartets are four interlinked meditations with the common theme being man's relationship with time, the universe, and the divine. In describing his understanding of the divine within the poems, Eliot blends his Anglo-Catholicism with mystical, philosophical and poetic works from both Eastern and Western religious and cultural traditions, with references to the Bhagavad-Gita and the Pre-Socratics as well as St. John of the Cross and Julian of Norwich.

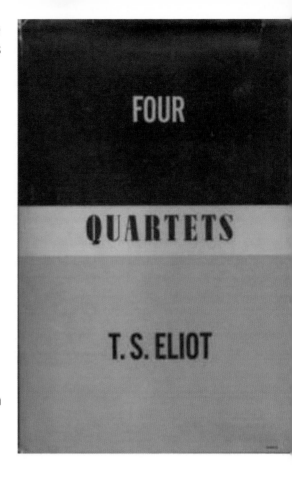

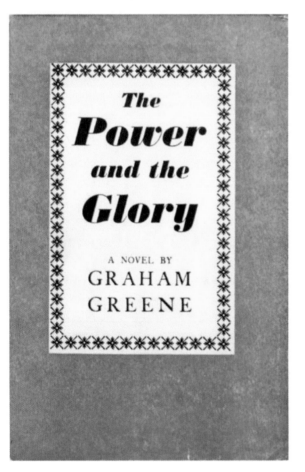

The Power and the Glory (1940) is a novel by British author Graham Greene. The title is an allusion to the doxology often recited at the end of the Lord's Prayer: "For thine is the kingdom, the power, and the glory, forever and ever, amen." It was initially published in the United States under the title The Labyrinthine Ways. Greene's novel tells the story of a renegade Roman Catholic 'whisky priest' (a term coined by Greene) living in the Mexican state of Tabasco in the 1930s, a time when the Mexican government was attempting to suppress the Catholic Church. That suppression had resulted in the Cristero War (1927-1929), so named for its Catholic combatants' slogan Viva Cristo Rey (long live Christ the King). In 1941, the novel received the Hawthornden Prize British literary award. In 2005, it was chosen by TIME magazine as one of the hundred best English-language novels since 1923. The main character is an unnamed 'whisky priest', who combines a great power for self-destruction with pitiful craveness, an almost painful penitence, and a desperate quest for dignity. By the end, though, the priest "acquires a real holiness." The other principal character is a police lieutenant tasked with hunting down this priest. This Lieutenant – also unnamed but thought to be based upon Tomás Garrido Canabal – is a committed socialist who despises the Church.

Fanny by Gaslight is the best known novel of Michael Sadleir. Written in 1940 and filmed in 1944, it is a fictional exploration of prostitution in Victorian London. In 1981 it was turned into a four-part BBC television series Fanny by Gaslight with Chloe Salaman in the title role.

Fanny (Phyllis Calvert) finishes at boarding school in 1880 and returns to London, where she witnesses Lord Manderstoke (James Mason) fight and kill her supposed father. She soon learns that her family has run a brothel next door to her home and (on her mother's death) that he was not her real father. She goes to meet her real father – a respected politician – and falls in love with Harry Somerford (Stewart Granger), his advisor. Manderstoke continues to thwart her happiness.

Michael Sadleir's best known novel was Fanny by Gaslight (1940), a fictional exploration of prostitution in Victorian London. It was adapted under that name as a 1944 film. The 1947 novel Forlorn Sunset further explored the characters of the Victorian London underworld. His writings also include a biography of his father, published in 1949, and a privately published memoir of one of his sons, who was killed in World War II.

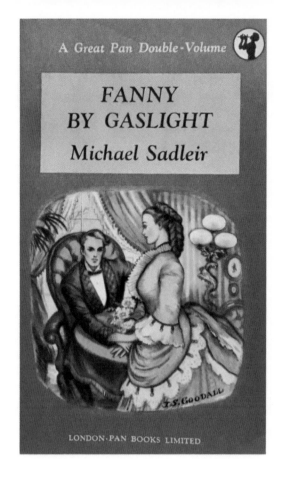

A *Great Pan Double-Volume*

FANNY BY GASLIGHT

Michael Sadleir

LONDON·PAN BOOKS LIMITED

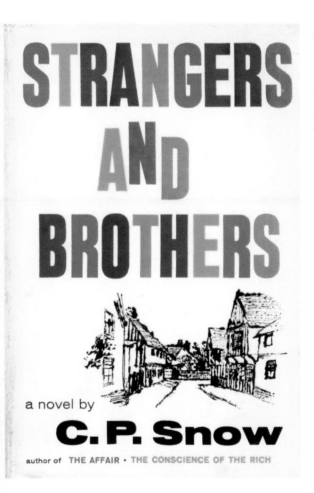

STRANGERS AND BROTHERS

a novel by

C. P. Snow

author of THE AFFAIR · THE CONSCIENCE OF THE RICH

Strangers and Brothers is a series of novels by C. P. Snow, published between 1940 and 1970. They deal with – among other things – questions of political and personal integrity, and the mechanics of exercising power. All eleven novels in the series are narrated by the character Lewis Eliot. The series follows his life and career from humble beginnings in an English provincial town, to reasonably successful London lawyer, to Cambridge don, to wartime service in Whitehall, to senior civil servant and finally retirement. The New Men deals with the scientific community's involvement in (and reaction to) the development and deployment of nuclear weapons during the Second World War. The Conscience of the Rich concerns a wealthy, Anglo-Jewish merchant-banking family. Snow analyses the professional world, scrutinising microscopic shifts of power within the enclosed settings of a Cambridge college, a Whitehall ministry, a law firm. For example, in the novels set in the Cambridge college a small, disparate group of men is typically required to reach a collective decision on an important subject. In The Masters, the dozen or so college members elect a new head by majority vote. In The Affair, a small group of dons sets out to correct a possible injustice: they must convince the rest of the college to re-open an investigation into scientific fraud.

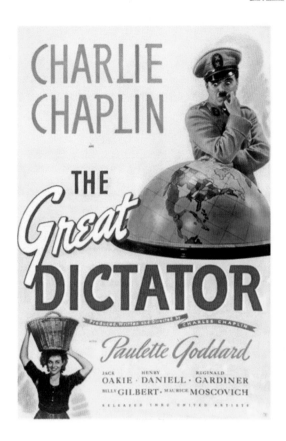

The Great Dictator. 20 years after the end of WWI, in which the nation of Tomainia was on the losing side, Adenoid Hynkel has risen to power as the ruthless dictator of the country. He believes in a pure Aryan state and the decimation of the Jews. This situation is unknown to a simple Jewish Tomainian barber who has been hospitalized since a WWI battle. Upon his release the barber, who had been suffering from memory loss about the war, is shown the new persecuted life of the Jews by many living in the Jewish ghetto, including a washerwoman named Hannah with whom he begins a relationship. The barber is ultimately spared such persecution by Commander Schultz, whom he saved in that WWI battle. The lives of all Jews in Tomainia are eventually spared with a policy shift by Hynkel himself, who is doing so for ulterior motives

Box Office
Budget:$2,000,000 (estimated)
Cumulative Worldwide Gross: $952,732

Run time is 2h 5mins

Trivia
Adolf Hitler banned the film in Germany and in all countries occupied by the Nazis. Curiosity got the best of him, and he had a print brought in through Portugal. History records that he screened it twice, in private, but history did not record his reaction to the film. Charles Chaplin said, "I'd give anything to know what he thought of it." For political reasons in Germany, the ban stayed after the end of WWII until 1958.

This film was financed entirely by Charles Chaplin himself, and it was his biggest box-office hit.

Released eleven years after the end of the silent era, this was Charles Chaplin's first all-talking, all-sound film.

According to documentaries on the making of the film, Charles Chaplin began to feel more uncomfortable lampooning Adolf Hitler the more he heard of Hitler's actions in Europe. Ultimately, the invasion of France inspired Chaplin to change the ending of his film to include his famous speech.

Goofs
(at around 30 mins) When the Jewish Barber has just returned to the Ghetto and is cleaning his windows, his white overcoat changes from buttoned to unbuttoned throughout the fight scene.

(at around 27 mins) When Hannah has tomatoes thrown at her by the soldiers, she has 3 prominent streaks of dirt on her right cheek as she cowers down to protect herself. When she gets up after the attack, the dirt is missing from her cheek.

(at around 30 mins) When the Jewish Barber cleans the word "Jew" off his shop window, a dotted line can be seen to mark where the W would be painted again for the next take.

The Shop Around The Corner. Alfred Kralik is the senior salesman in a long established Budapest gift shop, owned by the likeable and kindly Hugo Matuschek. Alfred has been there for 9 years and is very good at his job. One day a young woman, Klara Novak, comes into the shop looking for a job. They don't really have a position available but she impresses Mr. Matuschek with her skills and is taken on. Alfred and Klara don't get along very well but unbeknownst to either of them, they have been corresponding anonymously. On the day he is to meet her finally, Alfred is fired for reasons that are not clear to him. He has always gotten along well with Mr. Matuschek who it turn out, suspects him of having an affair with his wife. He's wrong of course but that evening, Alfred sees that Klara is the one he has been corresponding with. He's soon back in the shop as manager when Mr. Matuschek realizes his error but the question now is how he could possibly impress Klara without revealing who he is.

Box Office
Cumulative Worldwide Gross: $36,368

Run time 1h 29mins

Trivia

Soon after wrapping principal photography, Ernst Lubitsch talked to the New York Sun in January 1940. "It's not a big picture, just a quiet little story that seemed to have some charm. It didn't cost very much, for such a cast, under $500,000. It was made in twenty-eight days. I hope it has some charm."

To make sure his film was stripped of the glamour usually associated with him, Ernst Lubitsch went to such lengths as ordering that a dress Margaret Sullavan had purchased off the rack for $1.98 be left in the sun to bleach and altered to fit poorly.

James Stewart and Margaret Sullavan had known each other a long time before making this film. Both were in a summer stock company called the University Players. It was there that Stewart realized his potential as an actor, so he followed Sullavan and fellow player Henry Fonda to New York to begin an acting career in earnest.

Goofs

Before they leave the store room Alfred takes 5 boxes and Klara 4. In the next cut, suddenly Klara carries 5 boxes and Alfred has 4.

When Klara hurries out of the back room with her hat and coat she rushes past the rest of the employees as they enter the room in a group. Flora is the second-to-last person in the line and she is clearly inside the room before Klara runs past. In the next cut showing Klara hurrying through the store, Flora is the last person in line and is still in the doorway.

After dismissing his employees for the night, Mr. Matuschek sees Vadas leave the shop. As he watches him close the door, you can clearly hear off camera directions that sound like "turn" and "he's gone."

Rebecca. A young woman is in Monte Carlo, working as a ladies' companion, when she meets the recently-widowed, and very wealthy, Maxim De Winter. They fall in love and get married soon thereafter. The De Winters take up residence in Maxim's family estate, Mandalay. Mrs De Winter finds it hard to fit in.

The presence of Maxim's deceased wife, Rebecca, seems to permeate through the house and Mrs De Winter can't shake the feeling that she is constantly being compared to her and that she is an interloper.

Mrs. Danvers, Rebecca's personal maid, also takes care to make things as uncomfortable as possible for the new Mrs De Winter. Mrs De Winter has the constant fear that memories o Rebecca will drive her and Maxim apart. Over time, she grows to know more and more about Rebecca.

Box Office
Budget:$1,288,000 (estimated)
Cumulative Worldwide Gross: $72,275

Run time 2h 10mins.

Trivia
Because Sir Laurence Olivier wanted his then-girlfriend Vivien Leigh to play the lead role, he treated Joan Fontaine horribly. This shook Fontaine up quite a bit, so Sir Alfred Hitchcock decided to capitalize on this by telling her everyone on the set hated her, thus making her shy and uneasy, just what he wanted from her performance.

The first movie that Sir Alfred Hitchcock made in Hollywood, and the only one that won a Best Picture Oscar. Although it won Best Picture, the Best Director Award that year went to John Ford for The Grapes of Wrath (1940).

In order to maintain the dark atmosphere of the book, Sir Alfred Hitchcock insisted that this movie be shot in black and white.

Goofs
The word pamplemousse (French for grapefruit) is incorrectly spelled as 'pamplemouse' in the Princesse Hotel Monte Carlo menu toward the beginning of the film.

When Mrs. Danvers draws open the draperies in Rebecca's room, she tugs very slightly at the draw cord causing the huge drapes to open several feet.

The large map on the courtroom wall is a map of the Americas. It is grossly implausible that such a map would be on the wall of an English courtroom.

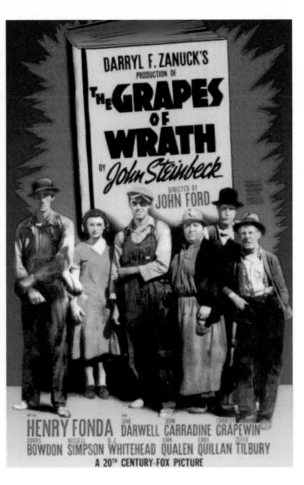

The Grapes Of Wrath. The Joad clan, introduced to the world in John Steinbeck's iconic novel, is looking for a better life in California. After their drought-ridden farm is seized by the bank, the family -- led by just-paroled son Tom -- loads up a truck and heads West. On the road, beset by hardships, the Joads meet dozens of other families making the same trek and holding onto the same dream. Once in California, however, the Joads soon realize that the promised land isn't quite what they hoped.

Winner of two Oscars in 1941 for:

Best Actress in a Supporting Role	Jane Darwell
Best Director	John Ford

Nominated for:
Best Picture	
Best Actor in a Leading Role	Henry Fonda
Best Writing, Screenplay	Nunnally Johnson
Best Sound, Recording	Edmund H. Hansen
Best Film Editing	Robert L. Simpson

Run time 2h 9mins uncut

Trivia

Prior to filming, producer Darryl F. Zanuck sent undercover investigators out to the migrant camps to see if John Steinbeck had been exaggerating about the squalor and unfair treatment meted out there. He was horrified to discover that, if anything, Steinbeck had actually downplayed what went on in the camps.

John Steinbeck was particularly enamoured with the performance of Henry Fonda as Tom Joad, feeling that he perfectly encapsulated everything he wanted to convey with this character. The two became good friends. Indeed Fonda did a reading at Steinbeck's funeral.

While filming the Joads' car traveling down the highway, John Ford wanted to add a shot showing the large number of caravans heading west, so the film's business manager stopped actual cars making the trek and paid the drivers five dollars to escort the Joads' jalopy for the cameras.

Goofs

One of the cars (License plate 263 with the silver bed springs sticking out the back) evacuating the Department of Agriculture camp site leaves the camp twice, once before the Joads pack up and once after.

In the beginning of the movie Grandma Joad is sitting at the table eating with a full set of teeth in her mouth. Later when they stop to buy the bread Pa Joad explains to the waitress that they need to soften the bread for Grandma to eat because she has no teeth.

Tom Joad's semi-retarded brother, Noah, vanishes after the swimming-in-the-river sequence. In the book, Noah believes he's a burden on the family and runs away. In the film, no explanation is given for his disappearance.

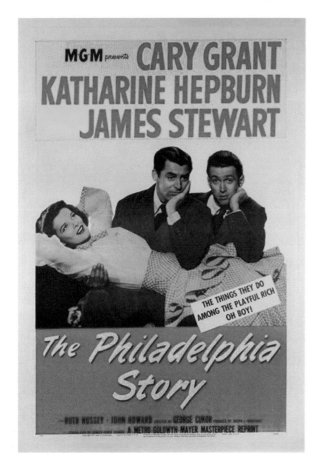

The Philadelphia Story. A Philadelphia socialite C.K. Dexter Haven as he's being tossed out of his palatial home by his wife, Tracy Lord. Adding insult to injury, Tracy breaks one of C.K.'s precious golf clubs. He gallantly responds by knocking her down on her million-dollar keester. A couple of years after the breakup, Tracy is about to marry George Kittridge, a wealthy stuffed shirt whose principal recommendation is that he's not a Philadelphia mainliner, as C.K. was. Still holding a torch for Tracy, C.K. is galvanized into action when he learns that Sidney Kidd, the publisher of Spy Magazine, plans to publish an exposé concerning Tracy's philandering father). To keep Kidd from spilling the beans, C.K. agrees to smuggle Spy reporter Macauley Connor and photographer Elizabeth Imbrie into the exclusive Lord-Kittridge wedding ceremony. How could C.K. have foreseen that Connor would fall in love with Tracy, thereby nearly lousing up the nuptials? As it turns out, of course, it is C.K. himself who pulls the louse-up, reclaiming Tracy as his bride.

Box Office
Gross USA: $404,524
Cumulative Worldwide Gross: $411,442

Run time 1h 52mins

Trivia

The film was shot in eight weeks, and required no retakes. During the scene where James Stewart hiccups when drunk, you can see Cary Grant looking down and grinning. Since the hiccup wasn't scripted, Grant was on the verge of breaking out laughing and had to compose himself quickly. Stewart (apparently spontaneously) thought of hiccupping in the drunken scene, without telling Grant. When he began hiccupping, Grant turned to Stewart saying, "Excuse me." The scene required only one take.

James Stewart never felt he deserved the Best Actor Oscar for his performance in this film, especially since he had initially felt miscast. He always maintained that Henry Fonda should have won instead for The Grapes of Wrath (1940), and that the award was probably "deferred payment for my work on Mr. Smith Goes to Washington (1939)."

Spencer Tracy turned down James Stewart's role because he was eager to make Dr. Jekyll and Mr. Hyde (1941).

Goofs

In the closing scene, a miscue by Grant and possible one by Hepburn, come off OK. Tracy opens a side door to announce to the guests that she and her fiancé "that was" have decided to call it a day. Dexter is standing behind her, and she says, "uh ... Dexter, what next?" He says "Three (sic) years ago I did you out of a wedding in this house by eloping to Maryland." She says to the guests, "Two years ago, uh, you were invited ..." She corrected the number of years which Grant clearly states wrongly - three, to two, but in catching and correcting his error, she got the rest of the line wrong.

As Connor and Tracy exit the library, the boom mic is reflected on the windshield of Tracy's car.

SHE LEARNED ABOUT MEN FROM HIM!

CARY GRANT
ROSALIND RUSSELL
in
HOWARD HAWKS'
"HIS GIRL FRIDAY"
RALPH BELLAMY
GENE LOCKHART
A COLUMBIA PICTURE

His Girl Friday. Four months after her resignation journalist Hildy Johnson returns to The Morning Post - just to tell her former boss and husband Walter Burns to stop bombarding her with telegrams, because she won't come back to him, and anyway, she is going to marry insurance agent Bruce Baldwin the next day. When Walter learns that Hildy and Bruce are going to Albany already in two hours, he has to act very quickly. He immediately starts a series of clever schemes to get Bruce out of the way and Hildy back to journalism. He knows that Hildy cannot resist an enticing commission. Earl Williams is a confused man, who is going to be executed the following day; if not The Morning Post succeeds in convincing the governor to pardon him. Hildy sees the possibilities to get a scoop by interviewing Williams, and postpones her departure some hours. She gets more and more entangled in the case, and even helps Williams to hide, when he has run away from prison. Soon she and Walter work feverishly side by side, and her fiancé Bruce just annoys her.

Box Office
Gross USA: $296,000

Run time 1h 32mins

Trivia

Rosalind Russell thought, while shooting, that she didn't have as many good lines as Cary Grant had, so she hired an advertisement writer through her brother-in-law and had him write more clever lines for the dialog. Since Howard Hawks allowed for spontaneity and ad-libbing, he, and many of the cast and crew didn't notice it, but Grant knew she was up to something, leading him to greet her every morning: "What have you got today?"

One of the first films (preceded by "Stage Door" (1937)) to have characters talk over the lines of other characters, for a more realistic sound. Prior to this, movie characters completed their lines before the next lines were started.

To maintain the fast pace, Howard Hawks encouraged his cast to add dialogue and funny bits of business and step on each other's lines whenever possible.

Goofs

When Bruce Baldwin comes to the press room late in the movie, an electric fan and small shelf on the wall to the left of the door both completely disappear. Both have been there in all previous scenes and both reappear after this scene.

After Walter's check-up, he puts his tie back on. At first, the skinny (back) end of the tie is longer than the wide (front) end. In the next shot, the front is properly longer than the back. When he goes to put his coat on, the back is longer than the front again.

When Walter goes to take Hildy and Bruce to lunch, his hat jumps from his right hand to his left hand between shots.

Waterloo Bridge. At the start of WWII, General Roy Cronin, standing mid-span of Waterloo Bridge in London as he is set to go off to war in France, recalls that exact place in a time during WWI when he met by chance the love of his life, Myra Lester. Then, he was an Army Captain, she a member of a ballet troupe and school, their meeting during an air raid. He was set to return to the trenches in France the following day, by which time they knew that they were the ones for each other, they wanting to get married before his departure so that she could live with his supportive upper crust mother, Lady Margaret Cronin. But issues in their respective lives threatened a happily-ever-after for them. For him, it is the hazards of battle and the possibility that he would never make it back alive. For her, it was the ballet troupe's strict and uncompromising head, Madame Olga Kirowa, who expected all her ballerinas to focus solely on ballet which meant no personal life. In Myra possibly needing to choose between the troupe or Roy and something else, that something else was never a certainty.

Box Office

Cumulative Worldwide Gross: $31,111

Run time 1h 48mins

Trivia

The scene in which Myra and Roy dance to "Auld Lang Syne" was supposed to have dialogue, but nobody could come up with the right words. At about 3:00 in the morning before shooting the scene was to take place, Mervyn LeRoy, a veteran of silent films, realized that there shouldn't be any lines and that the images should speak for themselves. The result is the most celebrated scene of the film.

Released a few months after the German and Soviet invasion of Poland, and in the middle of the invasion of France and the Low Countries, this is likely the earliest Hollywood film to include the Second World War in its plot.

Rita Carlyle played (uncredited) the Old Woman on Bridge in BOTH Waterloo Bridge (1931) & Waterloo Bridge (1940). It was the woman who dropped her basket of potatoes and cabbage in the earlier version and the flower lady in the later version.

Goofs

Even though the story takes place during the pre-1920 World War I period, all of Myra's clothes and hairstyles are strictly in the up-to-the-minute 1940 fashion.

When Roy and Myra are coming out of the Underground station after the air raid near the beginning of the film a traffic light is clearly visible in the top right hand corner. There were no traffic lights in London until 1931.

The uniforms worn by the officers are more like US uniforms in cut and cloth than British. Roy's officer's hat is distinctly American in shape.

The Mortal Storm. On January 30th, 1933 in a small village in southern Germany, Professor Roth celebrates his 60th birthday. It's also the day that Adolf Hitler becomes Chancellor of Germany. The professor is admired by his colleagues and students and much loved by his wife, stepsons Otto and Erich, and his daughter Freya. Otto, Erich and Freya's fiancé Fritz Marburg are all become avid Nazis and Professor Roth, who is a "non-Aryan", is soon sent to a concentration camp. Freya ends her engagement to Martin and she and her lifelong friend Martin Breitner soon fall in love. The oppressive regime forces Martin to flee to Austria and after the professor dies Freya and her mother try to flee but Freya is detained. Martin come to her rescue but they must escape a Nazi patrol that is tracking them down.

Soundtracks
Close Up the Ranks
(1864) (uncredited)
Written by S.F. Cameron
Sung by bar patrons

Run time 1h 40mins

Trivia

Nazi leader Adolf Hitler banned this film from release in Germany because of its strong anti-Nazi sentiments. In addition, all MGM films from that point until the end of the war were also banned in Germany because the studio made this one.

When this movie was made, America was not part of World War II. Most of the heads of the major studios in Hollywood were for American involvement in the war. This movie is one of a number made during the late 1930s and early 1940s that represented this belief. These films include A Yank in the R.A.F. (1941), Man Hunt (1941), Foreign Correspondent (1940), Confessions of a Nazi Spy (1939) and Sergeant York (1941).

Although the resolution of the story hinges upon Martin & Freya escaping from Germany, and crossing the border into Austria, before the film was even made, Austria had already become under Nazi control, and so their troubles would not have ended there, by any means.

At the start of the movie, Prof. Roth (Frank Morgan) is experiencing his 60th birthday. In fact, when Frank Morgan filmed that scene he was closer to his 50th birthday and unfortunately did not live in real life to see his 60th.

Margaret Sullavan, Jimmy Stewart, and Frank Morgan all starred in The Shop Around the Corner (1940), which was released just six months before this movie.

Goofs

Although the story takes place in 1933, Margaret Sullavan's hairstyle and clothing are strictly in the 1940 mode.

Fantasia. An innovative and revolutionary animated classic from Walt Disney, combining Western classical music masterpieces with imaginative visuals, presented with Leopold Stokowski and the Philadelphia Orchestra. The eight animation sequences are colourful, impressive, free-flowing, abstract, and often surrealistic pieces. They include the most famous of all, Paul Dukas's "The Sorcerer's Apprentice" with Mickey Mouse as the title character battling brooms carrying endless buckets of water. Also included are J.S. Bach's "Toccata and Fugue in D Minor"; Tchaikovsky's "Nutcracker Suite"; dinosaurs and volcanoes in Stravinsky's "Rite of Spring"; the delightful "Dance of the Hours" by Ponchielli with dancing hippos, crocodiles, ostriches, and elephants; and Mussorgsky's darkly apocalyptic "Night on Bald Mountain."

Box Office
Budget:$2,280,000 (estimated)
Gross USA: $76,408,097
Cumulative Worldwide Gross: $76,411,401

Run time 2h 5mins uncut

Trivia

Walt Disney himself related the story of a chance meeting with Leopold Stokowski at Chasen's restaurant. They agreed to have dinner together. As they talked, Disney told of his plans to do "The Sorcerer's Apprentice" and other possible projects using classical music with animation. Disney said that he was stunned when Stokowski, then one of the two most famous conductors in the country (the other being Arturo Toscanini), responded by saying, "I would like to conduct that for you." It was an offer he couldn't pass up.

Even after more than 60 years after its release, Disney still receives complaints from parents claiming the "Night on Bald Mountain" sequence terrified their children.

The animators secretly modelled elements of the Sorcerer in "The Sorcerer's Apprentice" on their boss, Walt Disney. The raised eyebrow was regarded as a dead giveaway. They call the character Yen Sid, which is "Disney", spelled backwards.

Goofs

The creatures gathered at the dinosaur water hole include animal's exclusive to different time periods. Stegosaurs lived only in the Jurassic Period, Ceratopsians only in the Cretaceous and Dimetrodons only in the Permian. It is possible that this was not yet known in 1940.

When introducing the "Pastoral" sequence, Deems Taylor mixes Greek and Roman names of deities: Bacchus, Vulcan and Diana are Roman; Zeus, Iris and Morpheus are Greek. Apollo is the only one who's Greek and Roman equivalents have the same name.

Sea Hawk. Geoffrey Thorpe is an adventurous and dashing pirate, who feels that he should pirate the Spanish ships for the good of England. In one such battle, he overtakes a Spanish ship and when he comes aboard he finds Dona Maria, a beautiful Spanish royal. He is overwhelmed by her beauty, but she will have nothing to do with him because of his pirating ways (which include taking her prized jewels). To show his noble side, he surprises her by returning the jewels, and she begins to fall for him.

When the ship reaches England, Queen Elizabeth is outraged at the actions of Thorpe and demands that he quit pirating. Because he cannot do this, Thorpe is sent on a mission and in the process becomes a prisoner of the Spaniards. Meanwhile, Dona Maria pines for Thorpe and when he escapes he returns to England to uncover some deadly secrets. Exciting duels follow as Thorpe must expose the evil and win Dona Maria's heart.

Box Office
Budget:$1,700,000 (estimated)

Run time 2h 7mins

Trivia

Henry Daniell couldn't fence. The climactic duel had to be filmed using a double and skilful inter-cutting.

The scenes of Doña Maria's carriage traveling through the countryside were taken from David Copperfield (1935). The film had to be darkened to disguise the fact that the carriage depicted was clearly too modern for this film's Elizabethan setting.

The Panamian sequences were deliberately tinted in sepia, as was done with the Kansas scenes in MGM's The Wizard of Oz (1939). Television prints of the film were entirely in black-and-white. The sepia was intended to suggest the sweltering heat of the jungles in Panama.

The beautifully crafted costumes were made for an Errol Flynn film from the previous year, The Private Lives of Elizabeth and Essex (1939). Reusing them saved Warner Bros. a huge amount of money, since the costumes were heavily researched, meticulously created and very expensive.

Goofs

At the beginning of the movie during King Phillip's monologue, the map on the wall shows western and northern parts of the North American continent which were not known at the time.

When what's left of Captain Thorpe and his men are coming back to their ship after being ambushed by the Spanish, you can see the shadow of a boom mic on the upper right portion of the ship on the screen.

The story takes place in 1588. The flint-lock muskets and pistols used in the film were not in use until two-hundred years later.

The Letter. Leslie Crosbie, the wife of a Malayan rubber plantation owner, shoots and kills a neighbour she claims had dropped in to see her unexpectedly and made improper advances towards her. Her husband Robert was away for the night and no one has any treason to disbelieve her. They must go to Singapore however where the Attorney General decides she must stand trial for murder.

She has strong support from the British expatriate community but her solicitor Howard Joyce learns from his clerk that Leslie had in fact written to the dead man asking him to visit her that evening. The original of the letter is in the hands of the dead man's Eurasian widow and she wants a hefty amount to part with it. Although she survives the trial, Leslie must pay a far greater price in the end.

Nominated for 7 Oscars

Box Office
Cumulative Worldwide Gross: $16,455

Run time 1h 35mins

Trivia

After shooting was completed, William Wyler watched a rough cut and decided that he wanted the character of Leslie to be more sympathetic. He ordered some re-writes and planned to shoot them. Bette Davis recalled - "I was heartbroken," she said, "As I felt, after reading the rewrites, that my performance could be ruined with these additions. I asked Willie if I could see the film before doing the retakes. To my horror I was crying at myself at the end of the showing. There was dead silence in the projection room when the lights came up. I said, 'If we film these retakes, we will lose the intelligent audience. It is impossible to please everyone with any one film. If we try to accomplish this, we can lose all audiences.' Plus, to my shame, even though I played the part, I deeply sympathized with Leslie Crosbie. We only made one small addition to the original film. Wyler had agreed with me. Thank God!"

In filming the opening murder scene, actor David Newell had to roll down the stairs eight times after being shot, before director William Wyler was satisfied with the scene.

Just months after the film was released, James Stephenson died suddenly of a heart attack at the age of 53.

Goofs

The motor vehicles throughout are all left-hand drive. In Singapore traffic drives on the left and all vehicles there are right-hand drive.

We see Leslie faint and taken to see the nurse. The nurse leaves the room and Leslie is talking to Howard Joyce, but behind Mr. Joyce is a shadow of a piece of equipment or crew visible on the room divider behind Mr. Joyce. The equipment is pulled back and the shadow disappears.

MUSIC 1940

Artist and songs that have been number one throughout the year and number of weeks at number 1.

Artist	Single	Reached number one	Weeks at number one
1940			
Frankie Masters	Scatter Brain	26th November 1939	8
Tommy Dorsey	All the thing Are Good	21st January 1940	2
Glenn Miller	In The Mood	4th February 1940	12
Glenn Miller	The Woodpecker Song	28th April 1940	7
Glenn Miller	Imagination	16th June 1940	3
Mitchell Ayers	Make Believe Island	7th July 1940	1
Glenn Miller	Fools Rush In	14th July 1940	1
Tommy Dorsey	I'll Never Smile Again	21st July 1940	12
Bing Crosby	Only Forever	13th October 1940	9
Artie Shaw	Frenesi	15th December 1940	13

Bing Crosby was the leading figure of the crooner sound as well as its most iconic, defining artist. By the 1940s, he was an entertainment superstar who mastered all of the major media formats of the day, movies, radio, and recorded music. Other popular singers of the day included Cab Calloway and Eddie Cantor.

Bandleaders such as the Dorsey Brothers often helped launch the careers of vocalists who went on to popularity as solo artists, such as Frank Sinatra, who rose to fame as a singer during this time. Sinatra's vast appeal to the "bobby soxers" revealed a whole new audience for popular music, which had generally appealed mainly to adults up to that time, making Sinatra the first teen idol. Sinatra's music mostly attracted young girls to his concerts. This image of a teen idol would also be seen with future artists such as Elvis Presley and The Beatles. Sinatra's massive popularity was also one of the reasons why the big band music declined in popularity; major record companies were looking for crooners and pop singers to attract a youth audience due to his success. Frank Sinatra would go on to become one of the most successful artists of the 1940s and one of the bestselling music artists of all time. Sinatra remained relevant through the 1950s and 60s, even with rock music being the dominant form of music in his later years. In the later decades, Sinatra's music would be mostly aimed at an older adult audience. Sinatra became one of the most respected and critically acclaimed music artists of all time.

Frankie Masters

"Scatter Brain"

"Scatter Brain" Frankie Masters was born on the 12th April 1904, USA. He began playing music while at college, eventually dropping out to become the leader of a theatre house band in Chicago, Illinois, USA. Several years later, in the late 20s, he decided to inaugurate his first dance band under his own name. Masters became a national celebrity when "Scatterbrain" became a major hit single, producing high profile engagements at the Pennsylvania Taft and Essex House hotels in New York. By the 40s they were among the most successful dance bands of their generation, with Masters acquiring a regular slot on Coca Cola Company's Victory Parade Of Spotlight Bands. After the end of World War II the band moved to the St. Francis Hotel in California, before returning to Chicago and the Stevens Hotel.

Tommy Dorsey

"All The Things Are Good"

"All the things are good". By 1939, Dorsey was aware of criticism that his band lacked a jazz feeling. He hired arranger Sy Oliver away from the Jimmie Lunceford band. Sy Oliver's arrangements include "On The Sunny Side of the Street" and "T.D.'s Boogie Woogie"; Oliver also composed two of the new band's signature instrumentals, "Well, Git It" and "Opus One". In 1940, Dorsey hired singer Frank Sinatra from bandleader Harry James. Frank Sinatra made eighty recordings from 1940 to 1942 with the Dorsey band. Two of those eighty songs are "In the Blue of Evening" and "This Love of Mine". Frank Sinatra achieved his first great success as a vocalist in the Dorsey band and claimed he learned breath control from watching Dorsey play trombone. In turn, Dorsey said his trombone style was heavily influenced by that of Jack Teagarden.

Glenn Miller

"In The Mood"

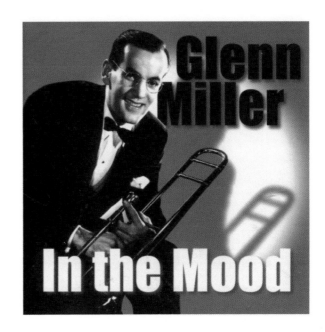

"I The Mood" **"**is a popular big band-era No. 1 hit recorded by American bandleader Glenn Miller. It topped the charts for 12 straight weeks in 1940 in the U.S. and one year later was featured in the movie Sun Valley Serenade. "In the Mood" is based on the composition "Tar Paper Stomp" by Wingy Manone. The first recording under the name "In the Mood" was released by Edgar Hayes & His Orchestra in 1938. "In the Mood" starts with a saxophone section theme based on repeated arpeggios that are rhythmically displaced; trumpets and trombones add accent riffs. The song was sold in 1939 to Glenn Miller, who experimented with the arrangement. The author of the final arrangement is unknown. One possibility is Eddie Durham because he wrote other arrangements on the same day that "In the Mood" was recorded.

Glenn Miller

"The Woodpecker Song"

"The Woodpecker Song". Is originally an Italian song. The music was written by Eldo Di Lazzaro in 1939, while the Italian lyrics were written by Bruno Cherubini. The English lyrics were written by Harold Adamson. The song became a hit in 1940, recorded by Glenn Miller and His Orchestra, The Andrews Sisters, and Kate Smith in 1940.

The Glenn Miller recording on RCA Bluebird featuring Marion Hutton on vocals reached #1 on the Billboard charts in 1940.

Glenn Miller

"Imagination"

"Imagination" is a popular song with music written by Jimmy Van Heusen and the lyrics by Johnny Burke. The song was first published in 1940. The two best-selling versions were recorded by the orchestras of Glenn Miller and Tommy Dorsey in 1940.

This was Glenn Millers third straight number one in the same year.

Mitchell Ayers

"Make Believe Island"

"Make Believe Island". In 1939, Bluebird Records offered the band an initial one-year contract; the arrangement lasted until 1942. All the while, the orchestra continued to function as a company, with the musician shareholders discussing business matters and voting on them. By 1940, the orchestra had its own show on CBS Radio. Ayres and the band appeared in three 1940s films: Swing time Johnny, Moonlight and Cactus, and Lady, Let's Dance.

Ayres and his orchestra reached the national number one spot for one week with their version of "Make Believe Island" (1940), vocal by Mary Ann Mercer.

Glenn Miller

"Fools Rush In"

"**Fools Rush In**". is a popular song. The lyrics were written by Johnny Mercer with music by Rube Bloom. The major hits at the time of introduction were Tony Martin, Glenn Miller with Ray Eberle, and Tommy Dorsey with Frank Sinatra. It was also recorded by Billy Eckstine. The song proved popular with 1960s pop and rhythm and blues artists, resulting in charted remakes in 1960 (Brook Benton), 1962 (Etta James), and 1963 (Ricky Nelson). The Ricky Nelson version was an enormous hit, reaching #12 on the Billboard pop chart and would become the most famous version of this song, and was featured in Kenneth Anger's film Scorpio Rising (1963). For their 1962 album Duet, Doris Day and André Previn recorded their interpretation of the song. Elvis Presley followed Ricky Nelson's style in 1971 as featured on the 1972 album Elvis Now.

Tommy Dorsey

"I'll Never Smile Again"

"**I'll Never Smile Again**" is a 1940 song written by Ruth Lowe. It has been recorded by many other artists since, becoming a standard.

The most successful and best-known version of the song was recorded by Tommy Dorsey and His Orchestra, with vocals provided by Frank Sinatra and The Pied Pipers. This recording was released as a Victor 78, 26628A, in 1940. This version was number one on Billboard's first "National List of Best Selling Retail Records" — the first official national music chart — on July 27, 1940, staying at the top spot for 12 weeks until October 12, 1940. The tune was inducted into the Grammy Hall of Fame in 1982.

Glenn Miller and His Orchestra also recorded a version of the song in 1940 on RCA Bluebird.

Bing Crosby

"Only Forever"

"Only Forever" is a song popularized in 1940 by Bing Crosby. It reached number one on the Billboard charts on October 19, 1940 and spent nine weeks in that position during a 20-week stay in the charts. "Only Forever" was written by James V. Monaco and Johnny Burke for the 1940 film Rhythm on the River and the song was nominated for the Academy Award for Best Original Song.

Crosby recorded it for Decca Records on July 3, 1940 with John Scott Trotter and His Orchestra. Tommy Dorsey and Eddy Duchin also enjoyed chart success with the song. The song has also been recorded by Anne Shelton, Dean Martin, Kay Starr, Nat King Cole, Vera Lynn and Al Bowlly & Jimmy Mesene.

Artie Shaw

"Frenesi"

"Frenesí" is a musical piece originally composed by Alberto Domínguez for the marimba, and adapted as a jazz standard by Leonard Whitcup and others. The word frenesí is Spanish for "frenzy".

A hit version recorded by Artie Shaw and His Orchestra (with an arrangement by William Grant Still) reached number one on the Billboard pop chart on the 21st December 1940, staying for thirteen weeks and was inducted into the Grammy Hall of Fame in 1982.

The Shaw recording was used in the soundtrack of the 1980 film Raging Bull.

WORLD EVENTS

January

1st | The Winter War, the Battle of Raate Road began. The Winter War was a military conflict between the Soviet Union (USSR) and Finland. It began with a Soviet invasion of Finland on the 30th November 1939, three months after the outbreak of World War II, and ended three and a half months later with the Moscow Peace Treaty on the 13th March 1940. The League of Nations deemed the attack illegal and expelled the Soviet Union from the organisation.

2nd | The Irish government introduced emergency powers to incarcerate members of the Irish Republican Army without trial.

3rd | U.S. President Franklin D. Roosevelt gave the 1940 State of the Union Address to Congress. "In previous messages to the Congress I have repeatedly warned that, whether we like it or not, the daily lives of American citizens will, of necessity, feel the shock of events on other continents. This is no longer mere theory; because it has been definitely proved to us by the facts of yesterday and today," the president said. He asked the Congress to approve increased national defence spending "based not on panic but on common sense" and "to levy sufficient additional taxes" to help pay for it.

7th | German documents record an attack on this date by the German First Minesweeper Flotilla on an unidentified submarine near Heligoland. Since the British submarine Seahorse was on patrol at the time but never returned, it is thought to have been sunk in this attack.

9th | During the war, Starfish, part of the 2nd Submarine Flotilla, conducted five uneventful war patrols in the North Sea. On the 9th January 1940, during her sixth patrol, she attacked a German minesweeper off Heligoland Bight, but after the attack failed and her diving planes jammed, Starfish was repeatedly attacked with depth charges. Badly damaged, she was forced to surface, and sank after all her crew were rescued by German ships.

January

11th | The Sergei Prokofiev ballet Romeo and Juliet made its Russian debut at the Korov Theatre in Leningrad amid wartime blackout conditions.

12th | The Danish tanker Danmark was torpedoed and sunk by the German submarine U-23 off the Orkney Islands. The crew of 40 escaped safely.

13th | The Finnish escort Aura II was sunk by its own depth charge trying to attack a Soviet submarine in the Sea of Åland.

14th | Hitler ordered that no one would be allowed to know more than he did about any secret matter.

17th | Europe was struck by a cold wave. In Finland the mercury dipped as low as −45 degrees Celsius, while in England the River Thames froze up for the first time since 1888.

19th | The British destroyer Grenville struck a mine in the Thames Estuary and sank. 77 lives were lost but 108 were rescued.

20th | Winston Churchill gave an address over the radio referred to as the "House of Many Mansions" speech, with neutral nations its primary subject. Churchill explained that there was "no chance of a speedy end" to the war "except through united action," and asked listeners to consider what would happen if neutral nations "were with one spontaneous impulse to do their duty in accordance with the Covenant of the League, and were to stand together with the British and French Empires against aggression and wrong?" Churchill concluded, "The day will come when the joy bells will ring again throughout Europe, and when victorious nations, masters not only of their foes but of themselves, will plan and build in justice, in tradition, and in freedom a house of many mansions where there will be room for all."

21st | The British destroyer Exmouth was sunk in the Moray Firth with the loss of all hands by the German submarine U-22.

23rd | Britain lowered the speed limit at night in populated areas to 20 miles per hour due to the sharp increase in the rate of auto accidents during blackouts.

24th | The German government ordered the registration of all Jewish-owned property in Poland.

January

25th France announced a new decree providing sentences of up to two years in prison and fines up to 5,000 francs for "false assertions" presented as "personal opinions" that correspond to "enemy propaganda and which, expressed publicly, indicate the marked intention of their authors to injure national defence by attacking the morale of the army and population."

26th U-boat captains were permitted from now on to make submerged attacks without warning on certain merchant vessels (though not on Spanish, Russian, Japanese or American ships) east of Scotland, in the Bristol Channel and in the English Channel.

27th The German government demanded at least 1 million industrial and rural workers be provided from Nazi-occupied Poland to work assignments in the Reich.

28th A new musical quiz show called Beat the Band premiered on NBC Radio. The audience sent in riddles to the house band in which the answer was always the title of a song. Listeners earned $10 if their question was used and an additional $10 if their question stumped the band.

29th Actress Jill Esmond won a divorce from her husband Laurence Olivier. Vivien Leigh was named as co-respondent and Olivier did not contest the proceedings.

30th Adolf Hitler gave a speech at the Berlin Sportpalast on the seventh anniversary of the Nazis taking power, his first formal address since narrowly avoiding the attempt on his life in November. The location of the speech was kept secret up until a few hours before it began. Hitler claimed that Britain and France "wanted war" and he vowed that they would "get their fight."

31st Britain secretly approached neutral Italy about purchasing badly needed fighter planes for the war effort. Germany would ensure that no such deal would be made.

February

1st Japan passed a massive budget devoting unprecedented sums to weapons and training.

3rd A German plane crashed on English soil for the first time in the war when a Heinkel He 111 was shot down near Whitby. Flight Lieutenant Peter Townsend of 43 Squadron was credited with the air victory.

5th The Anglo-French Supreme War Council met again in Paris with Neville Chamberlain and Winston Churchill in attendance. Franco-British plans for intervention in the Winter War were discussed.

6th The "Careless Talk Costs Lives" propaganda campaign began in Britain, aimed at preventing war gossip.

7th The Walt Disney animated film Pinocchio premiered at the Center Theatre in New York City.

8th Neville Chamberlain made a speech in Parliament updating the House on the general international situation, saying there was "no reason to be dissatisfied" with the early progress of the war. Chamberlain also praised the Finnish people for their "heroic struggle" that "has evoked the admiration of the world" and said that "further aid is now on its way."

9th   Joe Louis defeated Arturo Godoy by split decision at Madison Square Garden in New York City to retain the world heavyweight boxing title.

10th   From the south portico of the White House, U.S. President Franklin D. Roosevelt confronted a gathering of 4,500 members of the American Youth Congress, which had recently passed a resolution declaring that granting aid to Finland was an "attempt to force America into the imperialistic war" against the Soviet Union. Roosevelt told them that it was "a grand thing" for youth to be interested enough in government to come to Washington, but offered "some words of warning or perhaps I should say of suggestion ... do not as a group pass resolutions on subjects which you have not thought through and on which you cannot possibly have complete knowledge." The president continued, "That American sympathy is ninety-eight per cent with the Finns in their effort to stave off invasion of their own soil is by now axiomatic. That America wants to help them by lending or giving money to them to save their own lives is also axiomatic today. That the Soviet Union would, because of this, declare war on the United States is about the silliest thought that I have ever heard advanced in the fifty-eight years of my life. That we are going to war ourselves with the Soviet Union is an equally silly thought." The organization responded by booing the president, but the event was politically useful to Roosevelt in that it served as a rejoinder to accusations from his opponents that he was sympathetic to communism.

12th   German submarine U-33 was sunk in the Firth of Clyde by the minesweeper Gleaner. 25 of the crew perished but there were 17 survivors, one of which had three Enigma machine rotors in his pockets which were sent to Alan Turing at the Government Code and Cypher School for study.

13th   Finland asked Sweden to provide troops to fight against the Soviet Union, but Sweden refused out of fear that both Britain and Germany would respond by invading Sweden.

16th   In Egypt, the British Army created the 7th Armoured Division, later to be famous as the "Desert Rats".

17th   Germany accused Britain of "piracy, murder and gangsterism" over the Altmark incident and also lodged a protest with Norway demanding compensation for failing to protect the German ship within Norwegian territorial waters. Norway in turn protested to Britain for infringing on the country's neutrality.

21st   The results of a Gallup poll were published asking Americans, "If it appears that Germany is defeating England and France, should the United States declare war on Germany and send our army and navy to Europe to fight?" 77% said no and 23% said yes, not counting the 7% who expressed no opinion.

22nd   The Kriegsmarine launched Operation Wikinger, targeting British fishing vessels suspected of reporting the movements of German warships. En route, the destroyer flotilla was mistakenly bombed by a Heinkel He 111, sinking the Leberecht Maass and killing 280 aboard. The Max Schultz hit a naval mine attempting a rescue effort and also sank with the loss of all 308 crew.

24th   Speaking in his home city of Birmingham in an address broadcast to the United States, Neville Chamberlain outlined Britain's aims: the independence of the Poles and Czechs, and "tangible evidence to satisfy us that pledges and assurances when they are given will be fulfilled ... Therefore, it is for Germany to take the next step and to show us conclusively that she has abandoned that thesis that might is right."

February

25th	The first squadron of the Royal Canadian Air Force arrived in Britain.
26th	The large passenger liner RMS Queen Elizabeth left Clydebank on a secret maiden voyage to New York for her final fitting. The British generated false intelligence to make the Germans believe that the ship's destination was Southampton.
27th	Norway and Sweden refused to allow British and French troops to cross through their territory to aid Finland.
29th	The 12th Academy Awards were held in Los Angeles, hosted by Bob Hope for the first of what would be nineteen times. Gone With the Wind won eight awards including Best Picture. Hattie McDaniel became the first African-American to win an Oscar when she was named Best Supporting Actress. The Los Angeles Times published the names of the winners in its 8:45 p.m. edition, so most of the attendees already knew the results ahead of time. The Academy would respond by starting a tradition the following year in which the winners were not revealed until the ceremony itself when sealed envelopes were opened.

March

1st	In Germany, the second stop of U.S. Undersecretary of State Sumner Welles' fact-finding mission, he met with Joachim von Ribbentrop and listened to him speak almost non-stop for two hours. Welles came away thinking that Ribbentrop had a "completely closed mind" that was "also a very stupid mind."
2nd	Sumner Welles went to the Chancellery and met Adolf Hitler, who claimed to want peace but insisted that Britain was determined to destroy Germany. Welles' impression of Hitler was that he appeared to be calm and in excellent health and that "while his eyes were tired, they were clear."
3rd	Sumner Welles met Hermann Göring at Carinhall. Like Hitler, Göring blamed the war on Britain and France. Welles found Göring to be as cold and ruthless as the other Nazi leaders but thought he was at least capable of taking a broader view of international relations.
4th	The Home Office announced that women would not be asked to work more than 60 hours a week in British factories, and youth under 16 would not be required to work more than 48. In World War I, women were frequently working as many as 70 hours a week.
5th	In the English Channel, the Royal Navy seized seven Italian ships leaving Germany loaded with coal.
7th	The RMS Queen Elizabeth completed her secret maiden voyage from England to New York.
9th	Britain released the captured Italian coal ships and announced that Italy would be allowed to continue to import German coal, but only via overland routes.
11th	The French battleship Bretagne and cruiser Algérie departed Toulon with 147 tons worth of gold, bound for Canada where the French gold reserves would be kept for safekeeping.

March

12th Sumner Welles met Winston Churchill. In Welles' account of the meeting he wrote that "Mr. Churchill was sitting in front of the fire, smoking a 24-inch cigar, and drinking a whiskey and soda. It was quite obvious that he had consumed a good many whiskeys before I arrived." For almost two hours Welles listened to Churchill deliver "a cascade of oratory, brilliant and always effective, interlarded with considerable wit."

16th A British civilian was killed in a German air raid for the first time in the war when fourteen Junkers Ju 88 bombers attacked the British fleet at Scapa Flow.

18th Hitler met with Mussolini at the Brenner Pass in the Alps. Hitler made it clear that German troops were poised to launch an offensive in the west and that Mussolini would have to decide whether Italy would join in the attack or not. Since Italy was still not ready for war, Mussolini suggested that the offensive could be delayed a few more months, to which Hitler replied that Germany was not altering its plans to suit Italy. The two agreed that Italy would come into the war in due course.

21st The ocean liner Queen Mary departed New York City for Sydney to be refitted as a troopship.

RMS Queen Mary

23rd Twelve Irish Republican Army convicts rioted in HM Prison Dartmoor. The inmates took two warders prisoner, locked a third one in a cell and started a fire that took 90 minutes to put out.

24th The French destroyer La Railleuse was sunk off Casablanca by the accidental explosion of one of its own torpedoes. 28 crewmen were killed and 24 wounded.

March

25th | The British government ordered its troops not to participate in German radio broadcasts if they became prisoners of war. Britons had been tuning in to German radio to learn of the capture of family members by hearing their voices, long before information of their capture could reach the British government.

28th | The Anglo-French Supreme War Council met in London and agreed that neither Britain nor France would make a separate peace with Germany. The Council also agreed upon Operation Wilfred, a plan to lay mines in Norwegian coastal waters in the hopes of provoking a German response that would legitimize Allied "assistance" to Norway.

31st | Winston Churchill gave a speech over the radio titled "Dwelling in the Cage with the Tiger", a metaphor he used to describe the precarious geographical situation of the Dutch. As with his January 20 speech, Churchill primarily spoke about neutral countries and said, "It might have been a very short war, perhaps; indeed, there might have been no war, if all the neutral States, who share our conviction upon fundamental matters, and who openly or secretly, sympathize with us, had stood together at one signal and in one line. We did not count on this, we did not expect it, and therefore we are not disappointed or dismayed ... But the fact is that many of the smaller States of Europe are terrorized by Nazi violence and brutality into supplying Germany with the material of modern war, and this fact may condemn the whole world to a prolonged ordeal with grievous, unmeasured consequences in many lands." In the wake of the Altmark Incident and with Operation Wilfred about to go into action, Churchill said of Germany's neutral neighbours that "we understand their dangers and their point of view, but it would not be right, or in the general interest, that their weakness should be the aggressor's strength, and fill to overflowing the cup of human woe. There could be no justice if in a moral struggle the aggressor tramples down every sentiment of humanity, and if those who resist him remain entangled in the tatters of violated legal conventions."

April

1st | The BBC broadcast what appeared to be a speech by Adolf Hitler, in which the Führer reminded the audience that Columbus had discovered America with the help of German science and technology, and therefore Germany had a right "to have some part in the achievement which this voyage of discovery was to result in." This meant that all Americans of Czech and Polish descent were entitled to come under the protection of Germany and that Hitler would "enforce that right, not only theoretically but practically." Once the German Protectorate was extended to the United States, the Statue of Liberty would be removed to alleviate traffic congestion and the White House would be renamed the Brown House. CBS contacted the BBC in something of a panic trying to learn more about the origin of the broadcast, not realizing that it was an April Fools' Day hoax. The voice of Hitler had been impersonated by the actor Martin Miller.

2nd | Adolf Hitler signed the order for Operation Weserübung, the German invasion of Denmark and Norway.

3rd | The British cabinet approved Operation Wilfred, Winston Churchill's plan to mine the sea routes between Norway, Sweden and Germany and for Anglo-French landings in Norway to forestall a German invasion there, which British intelligence believed, was imminent. However, the British government still dithered about implementing the plan due to Norway's neutrality.

4th | Neville Chamberlain gave a speech to the Conservative Party in London stating he was confident of victory and that Hitler had "missed the bus" by not taking advantage of Germany's military superiority over Britain at the beginning of the war.

7th | British reconnaissance aircraft spotted a large German naval force heading northward. RAF bombers were dispatched to attack the group but this attack was not successful.

8th | The British destroyer Glowworm was sunk by the German cruiser Admiral Hipper in the Norwegian Sea. Despite being hopelessly outgunned, the Glowworm managed to ram the Admiral Hipper and inflict considerable damage before sinking. Captain Gerard Broadmead Roope (below) earned the first Victoria Cross of the war for his conduct, but it was only bestowed after the war when the Admiral Hipper's log describing the battle was read by the Royal Navy.

9th | The French and British put Plan R 4 into action. Plan R 4 was the World War II British plan for an invasion of the neutral states of Norway and Sweden in April 1940, in the event of Germany violating the territorial integrity of Norway. Earlier, the British had planned a similar intervention with France during the Winter War.

11th | First Lord of the Admiralty Winston Churchill made a speech to the House of Commons announcing that the strategically important Faroe Islands belonging to Denmark were now being occupied by Britain. "We shall shield the Faroe Islands from all the severities of war and establish ourselves there conveniently by sea and air until the moment comes when they will be handed back to the Crown and people of a Denmark liberated from the foul thraldom in which they have been plunged by the German aggression," Churchill said.

12th | The Alfred Hitchcock-directed psychological-thriller mystery film Rebecca premiered in the United States.

13th | Eight German destroyers and the submarine U-64 were sunk or scuttled during the Second Battle of Narvik.

April

15th | The British 146th Infantry Brigade landed at Namsos and started to advance south towards Trondheim. Further north, other British troops landed in the Lofoten Islands.

17th | The British cruiser Suffolk shelled a German held-airfield at Stavanger, but was attacked by aircraft in return, heavily damaged and put out of action for almost a year.

19th | At Verdal, British and German land forces engaged each other for the first time in the war.

20th | The British 148th Infantry Brigade arrived at Lillehammer and began moving south. The British supply base at Namsos came under bombing from German forces, but there was little the British could do to fight back as they were short on anti-aircraft weaponry.

23rd | On Budget Day in the United Kingdom, Chancellor of the Exchequer Sir John Simon announced that the government was seeking an all-time record £1.234 billion in revenue to meet the cost of the war through March 1941. Taxes and duties were increased on income, alcohol, tobacco, telephone calls, telegrams of "ordinary priority" and postage.

24th | Issue #1 of the comic book Batman was published, starring the character of the same name that was already popular from his appearances in other comics over the previous year. This first issue marked the debut of the Joker and Cat woman (initially called The Cat).

April

25th | Women gained the right to vote in the Canadian province of Quebec, the last province to grant women's suffrage.

26th | The British 15th Brigade fell back 3 kilometers to Kjorem after their supplies were destroyed by a full day of bombing from the Germans, who had complete air superiority. London began seriously considering a complete withdrawal from Norway.

27th | Germany finally declared war on Norway. Joachim von Ribbentrop took to the airwaves shortly afterward and claimed that the Germans had captured documents from the Lillehammer sector revealing a British and French plan to occupy Norway with Norwegian complicity. That same day Samuel Hoare made a radio address of his own in which he called Ribbentrop's assertion "despicable."

28th | The British government ordered troops at Trondheim to withdraw as the 15th Brigade fell back again to Dombås.

29th | The 1940 Summer Olympics, officially known as the Games of the XII Olympiad, were originally scheduled to be held from 21st September to 6th October 1940, in Tokyo, Japan. They were rescheduled for Helsinki, Finland, to be held from the 20th July to 4th August 1940, but were ultimately cancelled due to the outbreak of World War II. Helsinki eventually hosted the 1952 Summer Olympics and Tokyo the 1964 Summer Olympics.

30th | The British sloop Bittern was severely damaged off Namsos by German dive-bombers. Allied ships rescued the survivors and then scuttled the ship with a torpedo from the destroyer Janus.

May

1st | Adolf Hitler set a date of May 6 for the western offensive. This date would be postponed a few more times prior to May 10 due to weather.

3rd | The Allied evacuation at Namsos was completed, but German aircraft located part of the evacuation fleet and sank the destroyers Afridi and Bison.

4th | The Polish destroyer Grom was sunk in the fjord Rombaken by a German Heinkel He 111.

 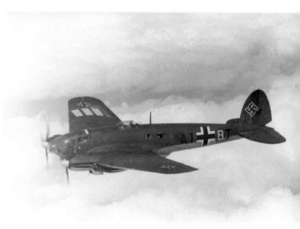

May

5th	RC Paris defeated Olympique de Marseille 2-1 in the Coupe de France Final.

5th — RC Paris defeated Olympique de Marseille 2-1 in the Coupe de France Final.

6th — Unemployment in the United Kingdom fell below 1 million people for the first time in 20 years.

7th — Norway Debate: The British House of Commons began a contentious debate on the conduct of the war. Sir Roger Keyes dramatically appeared dressed in full military uniform with six rows of medals and described in detail the government's mishandling of the Norwegian campaign. Leo Amery stood and uttered the famous words, "Somehow or other we must get into the Government men who can match our enemies in fighting spirit, in daring, in resolution and in thirst for victory." After quoting Oliver Cromwell, he continued: "I will quote certain other words. I do it with great reluctance, because I am speaking of those who are old friends and associates of mine, but they are words which, I think, are applicable to the present situation. This is what Cromwell said to the Long Parliament when he thought it was no longer fit to conduct the affairs of the nation: 'You have sat too long here for any good you have been doing. Depart, I say, and let us have done with you. In the name of God, go!'"

8th — The Norway Debate continued in Parliament. David Lloyd George said that since Chamberlain had asked the nation for sacrifice, "I say solemnly that the Prime Minister should give an example of sacrifice, because there is nothing which can contribute more to victory in this war than that he should sacrifice the seals of office." Chamberlain survived a motion of no confidence by a vote of 281 to 200, but the number of abstentions from within his own Conservative Party caused the level of support for his government to appear very weak.

9th — The age of conscription in the United Kingdom was raised to 36.

Germany invaded France and the Low Countries at dawn. The Battles of France, the Netherlands, and Belgium began. U.S. President Franklin D. Roosevelt learned of the German attack at 11:00 p.m. on the 9th May, Washington time. He phoned his Treasury Secretary, Henry Morgenthau, Jr., and told him to freeze Belgian, Dutch, and Luxembourger assets in the United States to keep them out of Germany's hands. Roosevelt could do little more that night, since phone calls to Paris and Brussels were rarely getting through, so he went to bed at 2:40 a.m. Neville Chamberlain went to Buckingham Palace around 6:00 in the evening (18:00) and resigned as Prime Minister of the United Kingdom. King George VI asked Winston Churchill to form the next government, and Churchill accepted.

12th — Child star Shirley Temple, through her mother Gertrude Temple, cancelled her movie contract with 20th Century Fox and retired from film acting at age 11.

13th — Winston Churchill made his first speech to the House of Commons as Prime Minister. He famously said, "I have nothing to offer but blood, toil, tears, and sweat."

14th — French artillery and antitank guns hit Erwin Rommel's tank near the Belgian village of Onhaye. Rommel was wounded in the right cheek by a small shell splinter as the tank slid down a slope and rolled over on its side, but he escaped serious injury.

15th — Churchill sent a message to Roosevelt asking for a one-year loan of forty or fifty older destroyers as well as aircraft, antiaircraft guns and steel. President Roosevelt sent a message back to Churchill explaining that a loan of destroyers would require an act of Congress, but generally agreeing on the other matters.

May

17th	The German 6th Army captured Brussels.
18th	Rommel's 7th Panzer Division captured Cambrai through deception. Rommel ordered his tanks and self-propelled guns to drive across the open fields and create as much dust as possible, creating the illusion that the advancing force was much larger than it actually was. The defenders abandoned the town without firing a shot.
19th	Winston Churchill made his first broadcast to the British people as Prime Minister. Churchill acknowledged that the Germans were making swift progress and that it would be "foolish ... to disguise the gravity of the hour," but said that only a "very small part" of the French Army had yet been heavily engaged. Churchill explained that he had formed an "Administration of men and women of every Party and of almost every point of view. We have differed and quarrelled in the past; but now one bond unites us all - to wage war until victory is won, and never to surrender ourselves to servitude and shame, whatever the cost and the agony may be." The speech was titled Be ye men of valour, after a quotation from 1 Maccabees in the Apocrypha.
21st	The Battle of Arras took place on the 21st May 1940, during the Battle of France in the Second World War. British and French tanks and infantry advanced south from Arras to force back German armoured forces, which were advancing westwards down the Somme river valley towards the English Channel, to trap the Allied forces in northern France and Belgium. The Anglo-French attack made early gains and panicked some German units but was repulsed after an advance of up to 6.2 mi (10 km) and forced to withdraw after dark to avoid encirclement.
22nd	Britain passed the Emergency Powers (Defence) Act 1940 putting banks, munitions production, wages, profits and work conditions under the control of the state.
24th	On Empire Day, King George VI addressed his subjects by radio, saying, "The decisive struggle is now upon us ... Let no one be mistaken; it is not mere territorial conquest that our enemies are seeking. It is the overthrow, complete and final, of this Empire and of everything for which it stands, and after that the conquest of the world. And if their will prevails they will bring to its accomplishment all the hatred and cruelty which they have already displayed."
25th	The British aircraft carrier Illustrious was commissioned.
26th	Benito Mussolini met with Army Chief of Staff Pietro Badoglio and Air Marshal Italo Balbo in Rome. Mussolini told them that Italy would have to enter the war soon if it wanted a place at the peace conference table when the spoils were divided up. Badoglio tactfully tried to explain that Italy was still unprepared for war, pointing out that there were not even enough shirts for all the soldiers. Mussolini snapped back, "History cannot be reckoned by the number of shirts." He set June 5th as the date for the Italian invasion of France.
27th	The Dunkirk evacuation codenamed Operation Dynamo began. The first 7,669 British troops were evacuated.
28th	Belgium surrendered unconditionally to Germany at 4 a.m. A bad-tempered Paul Reynaud announced in a radio address that day that "France can no longer count on the Belgian Army" and said the surrender had been made without consulting the British or French governments.

May

29th | The Germans captured Lille, Ostend and Ypres and 33,558 were evacuated from Dunkirk.

30th | In the wake of the previous day's losses, the British Admiralty ordered all modern destroyers to depart Dunkirk and leave 18 older destroyers to continue the evacuation. A total of 53,823 were evacuated on this day.

31st | Poor weather over Dunkirk allowed the British to conduct the day's evacuations with reduced fear of German air attacks. This day was the high point of the evacuation, with a total of 68,014 rescued.

June

1st | German bombers sank the French destroyer Foudroyant off Dunkirk as the evacuation from there continued. A total of 64,429 were evacuated on this day.

2nd | War Secretary Anthony Eden gave a radio address on the Dunkirk evacuation reporting that four-fifths of the British Expeditionary Force had been saved. "The British Expeditionary Force still exists, not as a handful of fugitives, but as a body of seasoned veterans," Eden said. "We have had great losses in equipment. But our men have gained immeasurably in experience of warfare and in self-confidence. The vital weapon of any army is its spirit. Ours has been tried and tempered in the furnace. It has not been found wanting. It is this refusal to accept defeat that is the guarantee of final victory." 26,256 were evacuated from Dunkirk as operations switched to only being undertaken at night due to the costly air attacks.

3rd | The last British troops were evacuated from Dunkirk.

4th | The Battle of Dunkirk ended with the overnight evacuation of 26,175 French troops. At 10:20 a.m. the Germans occupied the city and captured the 30–40,000 French troops who were left.

5th | The Germans began the second phase of the invasion of France, codenamed Fall Rot, by attacking across the Somme and Aisne rivers. The Germans initially met stiff resistance, since the French had spent the past two weeks organizing their defences south of the Somme.

7th | A single airplane from the French Navy bombed Berlin in a night raid. The Farman 223.4 lingered over the city for as long as possible to create the impression of more than one airplane, and then dropped its bomb load over some factories in Berlin's north end.

8th | The German 5th and 7th Panzer Divisions crossed the Seine River. The 5th Panzer Division captured Rouen.

9th | The French government fled Paris.

10th | At 6 p.m., Benito Mussolini appeared on the balcony of the Palazzo Venezia to announce that in six hours, Italy would be in a state of war with France and Britain. After a speech explaining his motives for the decision, he concluded: "People of Italy: take up your weapons and show your tenacity, your courage and your valour." The Italians had no battle plans of any kind prepared. Anti-Italian riots broke out in major cities across the United Kingdom after Italy's declaration of war. Bricks, stones and bottles were thrown through the windows of Italian-owned shops, and 100 arrests were made in Edinburgh alone.

June

11th Rommel's 7th Panzer Division reached Le Havre, then turned back to trap 46,000 British and French soldiers at Saint-Valery-en-Caux.

12th After a last stand, the outflanked 51st Highland Division and French 9th Army Corps surrendered to Rommel at Saint-Valery-en-Caux.

14th The first inmates of Auschwitz and Theresienstadt concentration camp arrived.

June

15th Operation Aerial was the evacuation of Allied forces and civilians from ports in western France from 15th to 25th June 1940 during the Second World War. The evacuation followed the military collapse in the Battle of France against Nazi Germany, after Operation Dynamo, the evacuation from Dunkirk and Operation Cycle, an embarkation from Le Havre, which finished on the 13th June. British and Allied ships were covered from French bases by five Royal Air Force fighter squadrons and assisted by aircraft based in England, to lift British, Polish and Czech troops, civilians and equipment from Atlantic ports, particularly from St Nazaire and Nantes.

The Luftwaffe attacked the evacuation ships and on the 17th June, evaded RAF fighter patrols and sank the Cunard liner and troopship HMT Lancastria in the Loire estuary. The ship sank quickly and vessels in the area were still under attack during rescue operations, which saved about 2,477 passengers and crew. The liner had thousands of troops, RAF personnel and civilians on board and the number of the passengers who died in the sinking is unknown, because in the haste to embark as many people as possible, keeping count broke down. The loss of at least 3,500 people made the disaster the greatest loss of life in a British ship, which the British government tried to keep secret on the orders of Winston Churchill, the British Prime Minister.

18th "This was their finest hour" was a speech delivered by Winston Churchill to the House of Commons of the United Kingdom on the 18th June 1940, just over a month after he took over as Prime Minister at the head of an all-party coalition government.

It was the third of three speeches which he gave during the period of the Battle of France, after the "Blood, toil, tears and sweat" speech of the 13th May and the "We shall fight on the beaches" speech of the 4th June. "This was their finest hour" was made after France had sought an armistice on the evening of the 16th June.

June

19th | Charles de Gaulle broadcast again over the BBC. "Faced by the bewilderment of my countrymen, by the disintegration of a government in thrall to the enemy, by the fact that the institutions of my country are incapable, at the moment, of functioning, I, General de Gaulle, a French soldier and military leader, realise that I now speak for France," he said. "In the name of France, I make the following solemn declaration: It is the bounden duty of all Frenchmen who still bear arms to continue the struggle. For them to lay down their arms, to evacuate any position of military importance, or agree to hand over any part of French territory, however small, to enemy control, would be a crime against our country. For the moment I refer particularly to French North Africa - to the integrity of French North Africa."

20th | The first Australian and New Zealand troops arrived in the United Kingdom.

21st | At about 3:15 p.m., peace negotiations between France and Germany began at the Glade of the Armistice in the Forest of Compiègne, using the same rail carriage that the Armistice of the 11th November 1918 was signed in. Adolf Hitler personally attended the negotiations at first, but left early as a show of disrespect to the French. A point of contention was the size of the zone that the Germans were to occupy, so the war dragged on for another day.

23rd | Adolf Hitler took a train to Paris and visited sites including the Eiffel Tower, the Arc de Triomphe and Napoleon's tomb at Les Invalides.

25th | German troops were issued English phrase books in preparation for an invasion of Britain.

28th | The Germans bombed the harbours of Saint Helier and La Roque on the island of Jersey and Saint Peter Port Harbour on Guernsey, killing a total of 42 people.

30th | The Germans occupied the Channel Islands unopposed.

July

1st | The British government advised women to conserve wood by wearing shoes with flatter heels.

3rd | Cardiff Blitz: the first German air raid on Cardiff, Wales took place.

4th | Winston Churchill expressed "sincere sorrow" as he delivered a speech to the House of Commons explaining "the measures which we have felt bound to take in order to prevent the French Fleet from falling into German hands."

6th | The first U-boat base in France became operational at Lorient.

9th | The British House of Commons unanimously passed a £1 billion war credit.

10th | The Battle of Britain began. In its opening phase the Luftwaffe attacked coastal targets and shipping convoys in the English Channel with the goal of reducing Britain's air defences and naval supply lines ahead of a general air offensive.

14th | Bastille Day in the unoccupied portion of France was observed solemnly with flags at half-mast.

July

19th Hitler made a speech to the Reichstag reviewing the course of the war and then warned, "Mr. Churchill, or perhaps others, for once believe me when I predict a great empire will be destroyed, an empire that it was never my intention to destroy or even to harm. I do realize that this struggle, if it continues, can end only with the complete annihilation of one or the other of the two adversaries. Mr. Churchill may believe this will be Germany. I know that it will be Britain." Hitler then appealed "once more to reason and common sense", saying, "I can see no reason why this war must go on." He said if Churchill brushed aside this appeal, "I shall have relieved my conscience in regard to the things to come."

20th The British government banned the buying and selling of new cars.

23rd Chancellor of the Exchequer Sir Kingsley Wood introduced Britain's third war budget. A 24 percent tax was imposed on luxuries.

24th The French passenger liner Meknés departed Southampton for Marseilles for repatriation of the 1,277 captured French Navy sailors aboard. The ship was torpedoed in the English Channel by the German torpedo boat S-27 despite the Meknés' displays of neutrality. Four British destroyers rescued the survivors but 416 perished.

25th A British coal convoy took heavy losses from German dive bombers. The Admiralty ordered future convoys to take place at night as a result.

27th Bugs Bunny made his debut in the animated short, A Wild Hare.

28th German fighter ace Werner Mölders was wounded in the legs by enemy fire during the Battle of Britain but managed to return to base at Wissant. Mölders spent the next month recovering in hospital.

29th German naval command issued a memo noting that the mid-September 1940 date for an invasion of Britain as demanded by Hitler was possible, but recommended a postponement to May 1941.

31st A conference was held at the Berghof between Hitler, Keitel, Jodl, Raeder, Brauchitsch, Halder and Puttkamer. Raeder reported that the navy would not be ready for Operation Sea Lion until mid-September, if then, so discussion turned to attacking the Soviet Union instead. Hitler believed that defeating Russia would make Germany unbeatable and force Britain to come to terms, so an invasion of the Soviet Union was set for spring 1941.

August

1st Hitler issued Directive No. 17, declaring his intention to intensify air and sea warfare against the English in order to "establish the necessary conditions for the final conquest of England."

4th American General John J. Pershing gave a nationwide radio broadcast urging that aid be sent to Britain. "It is not hysterical to insist that democracy and liberty are threatened," Pershing said. "Democracy and liberty have been overthrown on the continent of Europe. Only the British are left to defend democracy and liberty in Europe. By sending help to the British we can still hope with confidence to keep the war on the other side of the Atlantic Ocean, where the enemies of liberty, if possible, should be defeated."

August

7th Winston Churchill and Charles de Gaulle signed an agreement on the military organization of the Free French. Churchill agreed to allow the French units to have as much autonomy as possible.

9th The first air raid of the Birmingham Blitz took place when a single aircraft bombed Erdington.

12th The second phase of the Battle of Britain began as the Luftwaffe expanded its targets to include British airfields. Bf 110s and Stuka dive bombers attacked radar installations along the coastlines of Kent, Sussex and the Isle of Wight, damaging five radar stations and putting one out of action for eleven days.

13th The German military operation known as Adlertag was put into action with the goal of destroying the Royal Air Force, but the attempt failed.

15th In the biggest air engagement of the Battle of Britain up to this point, the Luftwaffe attempted to overwhelm the RAF with a series of major air attacks. The Germans lost 76 aircraft to the British 34, and to the Germans the day became known as Black Thursday.

16th The Spanish Surrealist artist Salvador Dalí and wife Gala arrived in New York to escape the war in Europe. They would not return to Europe for eight years.

17th Adolf Hitler ordered a total blockade of Britain as a means of weakening the island prior to Operation Sea Lion.

18th In the Battle of Britain the air battle known as The Hardest Day was fought, with an inconclusive result. The Germans lost 69 aircraft and the British 29. The Hardest Day is a name given to a Second World War air battle fought on the 18th August 1940 during the Battle of Britain between the German Luftwaffe and British Royal Air Force. On this day, the Luftwaffe made an all-out effort to destroy RAF Fighter Command. The air battles that took place on this day were amongst the largest aerial engagements in history to that time. Both sides suffered heavy losses. In the air, the British shot down twice as many Luftwaffe aircraft as they lost. However, many RAF aircraft were destroyed on the ground, equalising the total losses of both sides. Further large and costly aerial battles took place after the 18th August, but both sides lost more aircraft combined on this day than at any other point during the campaign, including the 15th September, the Battle of Britain Day, generally considered the climax of the fighting. For this reason, the 18th August 1940 became known as "the Hardest Day" in Britain.

August

19th The weather in Britain from this day through to August 23rd was wet with plenty of low cloud, causing a drop in the frequency of air raids. British ground crews took advantage of the lull in the fighting to repair damaged planes and airfields while Hermann Göring fumed at the loss of time.

20th "Never was so much owed by so many to so few" was a wartime speech made by the British prime minister Winston Churchill on the 20th August 1940. The name stems from the specific line in the speech, Never in the field of human conflict was so much owed by so many to so few, referring to the ongoing efforts of the Royal Air Force crews who were at the time fighting the Battle of Britain, the pivotal air battle with the German Luftwaffe with Britain expecting an invasion. Pilots who fought in the battle have been known as The Few ever since; at times being specially commemorated on the 15th September, "Battle of Britain Day".

22nd Harrow in northwest London received a German bomb at 3:30 a.m., the first to fall within the borders of the London Civil Defence Area.

23rd King George VI commanded that the names of all Germans and Italians be stricken from the lists of British titles and decorations. The order affected Benito Mussolini, who had been made a member of the Order of the Bath in 1923, as well as King Victor Emmanuel III who had been a member of the Order of the Garter. No prominent Nazis were affected as few Germans held any British titles.

24th The Luftwaffe dropped bombs on the financial heart of London and Oxford Street in the West End, probably unintentionally as the German bomber pilots had likely made a navigational error and did not know they were over the city. Winston Churchill was outraged at what he perceived to be a deliberate attack and ordered the RAF to bomb Berlin in retaliation.

25th The RAF bombed Berlin for the first time in the war. Damage was slight and nobody was killed, but it came as a loss of face for Hermann Göring, who had boasted that Berlin would never be bombed. Hitler authorized the bombing of London in retaliation.

26th No. 1 Fighter Squadron RCAF became the first Royal Canadian Air Force unit to engage enemy planes in battle when it encountered German bombers over southern England.

27th President Roosevelt signed a joint resolution authorizing him to call National Guard and Army Reserve components into federal service for one year.

28th The first major air raid on Liverpool took place in August 1940, when 160 bombers attacked the city on the night of the 28th August.

This assault continued over the next three nights, then regularly for the rest of the year. There were 50 raids on the city during this three-month period. Some of these were minor, comprising a few aircraft, and lasting a few minutes, with others comprising up to 300 aircraft and lasting over ten hours. On the 18th September, 22 inmates at Walton Gaol were killed when high-explosive bombs demolished a wing of the prison.

31st Film stars Laurence Olivier and Vivien Leigh were married at the San Ysidro Ranch in California.

September

1st | Biggin Hill aerodrome in Kent was heavily damaged by a German bombing raid.

4th | Hitler told a crowd at a rally in Berlin: "When the British air force drops two or three or four thousand kilograms of bombs, then we will in one night drop 150, 230, 300 or 400 thousand kilograms - we will raise their cities to the ground."

5th | Oil storage tanks at Thameshaven were among the day's targets of German bombers. Fires broke out at Thameshaven that could be seen from London.

8th | The Blitz began when the Luftwaffe shifted its focus from bombing British airfields and aircraft factories to conducting terror raids on London and other major cities in an effort to break the morale of the British people. This proved to be a mistake, as it would give RAF Fighter Command much-needed time to regroup.

11th | Winston Churchill gave a radio address saying that a German invasion of Britain could not be delayed for much longer if it was to be tried at all, so "we must regard the next week or so as a very important week for us in our history. It ranks with the days when the Spanish Armada was approaching the Channel and Drake was finishing his game of bowls, or when Nelson stood between us and Napoleon's Grand Army at Boulogne. We have read about all this in the history books, but what is happening now is on a far greater scale and of far more consequence to the life and future of the world and its civilization than those brave old days of the past. Every man and woman will therefore prepare himself and herself to do his duty whatever it may be, with special pride and care."

12th | U.S. Ambassador to Tokyo Joseph Grew warned Secretary of State Hull that Japan might treat an American embargo on oil exports as sanctions and retaliate.

15th | The large-scale air battle known as Battle of Britain Day was fought. Believing the RAF was near its breaking point, the Luftwaffe mounted an all-out offensive, sending two huge waves of about 250 bombers each to bomb London and surrounding areas. The RAF managed to scatter many of the German bomber formations and shoot down 61 planes while losing 31 in return, inflicting a clear and decisive defeat on the Germans.

16th | RAF planes from the carrier Illustrious attacked Benghazi and sank four Italian ships.

17th | Heinrich Himmler ruled that all Polish workers must wear a yellow badge marked with the letter "P" to distinguish themselves from Germans.

19th | The Royal Air Force bombed German invasion barges in ports along the French coast. After the attack, Hitler ordered the barges dispersed.

21st | The British government officially approved the use of the London Underground as an air-raid shelter, long after civilians had started using it as one anyway.

25th | Joachim von Ribbentrop alerted the German embassy in the Soviet Union that Japan was likely to join Italy and Germany in an alliance soon. Should this happen, the ambassador was instructed to reassure Moscow that this alliance was meant to deter the United States from entering the war and was not directed against Soviet interests?

September

26th | The U.S. government placed an embargo on the exportation of scrap iron and steel to any country outside the Western Hemisphere excluding Britain, effective from the 16th October.

27th | The Tripartite Pact, also known as the Berlin Pact, was an agreement between Germany, Italy and Japan signed in Berlin on the 27th September 1940 by, respectively, Joachim von Ribbentrop, Galeazzo Ciano and Saburō Kurusu. It was a defensive military alliance that was eventually joined by Hungary (20th November 1940), Romania (23rd November 1940), Bulgaria (1st March 1941) and Yugoslavia (25th March 1941), as well as by the German client state of Slovakia (24th November 1940). Yugoslavia's accession provoked a coup d'état in Belgrade two days later, and Germany, Italy and Hungary responded by invading Yugoslavia (with Bulgarian and Romanian assistance) and partitioning the country. The resulting Italo-German client state known as the Independent State of Croatia joined the pact on the 15th June 1941.

28th | The first U.S. destroyers reached Britain.

29th | British warships bombarded the coastal road of Italian Libya.

30th | The day before the annual two-week autumn vacation, school children in Berlin were told that they would be granted extra vacation time if their parents wanted them to go to the country or accept invitations from relatives in rural areas.

October

3rd | Neville Chamberlain stepped down as Lord President of the Council due to failing health.

4th | Adolf Hitler and Benito Mussolini met at the Brenner Pass to discuss a strategy that included the possibility of Francoist Spain entering the war on their side. Mussolini had already decided to attack Greece and hinted at his intention by speaking scornfully of the attitude of the "double-dealing" Greek government, but Hitler brushed such talk aside and said that the Axis powers should avoid any initiative that was not "absolutely useful." Hitler did not reveal his intention to attack the Soviet Union.

6th	Mussolini made a surprise inspection of armed forces in northern Italy as the Fascist press predicted that "something big" was coming soon.
7th	The Royal Air Force conducted its heaviest raid on Berlin to date.
8th	The John Ford-directed drama film The Long Voyage Home starring John Wayne, Thomas Mitchell and Ian Hunter premiered at the Rivoli Theatre in New York City.
9th	Winston Churchill was elected head of the Conservative Party following the retirement of Neville Chamberlain.
11th	The British battleship Revenge and six destroyers bombarded Cherbourg. Philippe Pétain gave a radio address suggesting to the French people that they reconsider their historic view of who was friend and who was foe among the European nations.
13th	14-year old Princess Elizabeth made her first public speech, a radio address to the children of the British Commonwealth. Her ten-year-old sister Princess Margaret joined in at the end.
14th	A German bomb exploded on the road above Balham station in south London, creating a large crater which a double-decker bus drove into during blackout conditions. A total of 66 people were killed and pictures of the bus in the crater were published around the world.

October

16th | Two Air Raid Precautions rescue workers were jailed for one year each at the Old Bailey for looting after they took £16 they found in a bombed-out house.

20th | Italian planes attacked oilfields in Bahrain and Saudi Arabia.

21st | Winston Churchill made a radio broadcast directed to the people of France. In a French-language address he appealed to them not to hinder Britain in the war against Germany, saying that "we are persevering steadfastly and in good heart in the cause of European freedom and fair dealing for the common people of all countries for which, with you, we draw the sword ... Remember, we shall never stop, never weary, and never give in, and that our whole people and empire have bowed themselves to the task of cleansing Europe from the Nazi pestilence and saving the world from the new Dark Ages."

23rd | President Roosevelt made a campaign speech in Philadelphia in which he answered many charges from his opponents, including one in particular that he called "outrageously false ... a charge that offends every political and religious conviction that I hold dear. It is the charge that this Administration wishes to lead this country into war." Roosevelt's speech concluded: "We are arming ourselves not for any foreign war. We are arming ourselves not for any purpose of conquest or intervention in foreign disputes. I repeat again that I stand on the platform of our party; 'We will not participate in foreign wars and will not send our Army, naval or air forces to fight in foreign lands outside of the Americas except in case of attack.' It is for peace that I have laboured; and it is for peace that I shall labour all the days of my life."

25th | The Royal Air Force bombed Hamburg and Berlin.

28th | Hitler and Mussolini met in Florence to exchange the latest war information. Hitler might have intended to use the meeting to dissuade Mussolini from attacking Greece had the invasion not, as it turned out, gone ahead that morning. Mussolini was in high spirits and told Hitler, "Don't worry, in two weeks, it will all be over." Hitler wished Mussolini the best of luck and refrained from expressing any disapproval, though after the meeting he fumed to his inner circle that what Mussolini had done was "pure madness" and that he should have attacked Malta instead.

29th | The British occupied Crete and began to mine the waters around Greece.

31st | The Battle of Britain ended. Between August 8 and this date the Luftwaffe lost 2,375 planes while the RAF lost 800.

November

2nd | One of the most extraordinary aviation incidents of the war took place. Greek Air Force pilot Marinos Mitralexis, after running out of ammunition, rammed an Italian bomber. Mitralexis then landed his plane and captured the Italian crew who had parachuted to safety.

3rd | After enduring 57 consecutive nights of bombing since the Blitz began, London went a night without being bombed.

November

4th | Operation MB8 was a British Royal Navy operation in the Mediterranean Sea from the 4th to the 11th November 1940. It was made up of six forces comprising two aircraft carriers, five battleships, 10 cruisers and 30 destroyers, including much of Force H from Gibraltar, protecting four supply convoys.

5th | The German heavy cruiser Admiral Scheer located Allied convoy HX 84 in the North Atlantic and sank the British armed merchant cruiser Jervis Bay and five cargo ships.

7th | Irish Taoiseach Éamon de Valera rejected a British request that strategic naval ports and air bases on Irish territory be rendered or leased to Britain.

10th | The first aircraft to be ferried from Gander, Newfoundland to the United Kingdom took off. The formation of seven Lockheed Hudson bombers landed the next morning at Aldergrove, Northern Ireland after a 10-hour-17-minute flight. Over the course of the war some 10,000 aircraft would travel this route from North America to Europe.

11th | The Battle of Taranto began off Taranto, Italy. The Royal Navy launched the first all-aircraft ship-to-ship naval attack in history.

13th | The Handley Page Halifax is a British Royal Air Force four-engine heavy bomber of the Second World War. It was developed by Handley Page to the same specification as the contemporary twin-engine Avro Manchester.

November

14th	The Nazis legalized the human consumption of dog meat within the German Reich, effective from the 1st January.
16th	The RAF bombed Berlin, Hamburg, Bremen and other cities in retaliation for the Coventry bombing.
17th	The British attempted Operation White, an attempt to deliver fourteen aircraft from the carrier HMS Argus to Malta, but only five planes made it due to bad weather and the presence of the Italian Fleet.
19th	About 900 people were killed in a German bombing raid on Birmingham.
22nd	All Star Comics #3 was published, marking the debut of the first team of superheroes, the Justice Society of America.
23rd	Southampton Blitz: The first sustained air raid on Southampton occurred. 77 were killed and more than 300 injured.
25th	Woody Woodpecker made his debut in the animated short, Knock Knock.
26th	In the wake of the German–Soviet Axis talks, Vyacheslav Molotov told the German ambassador to the Soviet Union that the USSR was willing to join a four-power pact with Germany, Italy and Japan if new Soviet territorial demands were met, including expansion into the Persian Gulf and the annexation of Finland. Hitler called Stalin a "cold-blooded blackmailer" and refused to make any response to the Soviet proposal.
28th	The Germans bombed Liverpool and killed 166 civilians when a parachute mine caused a blast of boiling water and gas in an underground shelter.
29th	German military leaders issued a draft plan for the German invasion of the Soviet Union.
30th	A six-hour attack occurred in the Southampton Blitz, killing 137 people.

December

1st	Allied convoy HX 90 was sighted by German submarine U-101. The Germans would sink a total of 11 ships from the convoy from this day through to December 3rd.
2nd	The British armed merchant cruiser Forfar was sunk west of Scotland by the German submarine U-99. The cargo ship Wilhelmina was torpedoed and sunk in the North Atlantic by the German submarine U-94.
4th	The swashbuckler film The Son of Monte Cristo starring Louis Hayward and Joan Bennett premiered at the Capitol Theatre in New York City.
6th	British submarine HMS Regulus was lost near Taranto, probably to a naval mine.
7th	The British Fairey Barracuda dive bomber plane had its first test flight.

December

7th | Ambassador Alfieri met with Adolf Hitler, who gave him a second lecture against Italy attacking Greece. Hitler said that Mussolini should resort to mobile courts-martial and executions if he wanted to turn the situation around. Hitler did agree to authorize fifty heavy troop transport planes to move fresh units from Italy to Albania.

8th | The British passenger and cargo steamship Calabria was torpedoed and sunk by the German submarine U-103 off County Galway, Ireland.

9th | Operation Compass was the first large Allied military operation of the Western Desert Campaign (1940–1943) during the Second World War. British and other Commonwealth and Allied forces attacked Italian forces in western Egypt and Cyrenaica, the eastern province of Libya, from December 1940 to February 1941. The Western Desert Force (Lieutenant-General Richard O'Connor) with about 36,000 men, advanced from Mersa Matruh in Egypt on a five-day raid against the Italian positions of the 10th Army (Marshal Rodolfo Graziani), which had about 150,000 men in fortified posts around Sidi Barrani in Egypt and in Cyrenaica.

The 10th Army was swiftly defeated and the British continued the operation, pursuing the remnants of the 10th Army to Beda Fomm and El Agheila on the Gulf of Sirte. The British took over 138,000 Italian and Libyan prisoners, hundreds of tanks, and more than 1,000 guns and aircraft, against British losses of 1,900 men killed and wounded, about 10 per cent of the infantry. The British were unable to continue beyond El Agheila, due to broken down and worn out vehicles and the diversion, beginning in March 1941, of the best-equipped units to the Greek Campaign in Operation Lustre.

12th | The first of four nights of heavy German bombing of Sheffield, England known as the Sheffield Blitz began.

14th | Plutonium was first isolated and produced at the University of California, Berkeley.
German submarine U-71 was commissioned.

15th | The ashes of Napoleon II were brought from Vienna to Paris, exactly one hundred years to the day since the retour des cendres when Napoleon Bonaparte's repatriated remains were interred at Les Invalides. The move was meant as a gesture of reconciliation on the part of Hitler, but a popular joke among the French went that the Parisians would have preferred coal to ashes.

16th | Bombing of Mannheim: The first area bombardment of a German city was conducted by the Royal Air Force when 134 bombers attacked Mannheim during the night, starting large fires on both banks of the Rhine.

17th | U.S. President Franklin D. Roosevelt gave a press conference in which he suggested leasing or selling of arms to Britain "on the general theory that it may still prove true that the best defence of Great Britain is the best defence of the United States, and therefore that these materials would be more useful to the defence of the United States if they were used in Great Britain, than if they were kept in storage here."

19th | German submarine U-37 mistakenly torpedoed and sank the Vichy French submarine Sfax and support ship Rhône off the coast of Morocco. The U-boat captain chose not to record this incident on the ship's logs.

December

20th Two Spitfire fighters of No. 66 Squadron RAF attacked Le Touquet in France, strafing targets of opportunity such as power transformers. This tactic, codenamed Rhubarb, marked a shift in RAF tactics to a more offensive role.

21st The RAF bombed docks and oil tanks at Porto Marghera, Italy.

22nd The heaviest raids of the Manchester Blitz began. Over the next two days a total of 654 people were killed and over 2,000 injured.

23rd Winston Churchill broadcast an appeal to the people of Italy, telling them to overthrow Mussolini for bringing them into a war against their wishes. "Surely the Italian army, which has fought so bravely on many occasions in the past but now evidently has no heart for the job, should take some care of the life and future of Italy?" Churchill asked. It is unlikely that many Italians heard the speech since they were forbidden from listening to foreign broadcasts.

24th Mahatma Gandhi wrote his second letter to Hitler, addressing him as "Dear Friend" and appealing to him "in the name of humanity to stop the war. You will lose nothing by referring all the matters of dispute between you and Great Britain to an international tribunal of your joint choice. If you attain success in the war, it will not prove that you were in the right. It will only prove that your power of destruction was greater. Whereas an award by an impartial tribunal will show as far as it is humanly possible which party was in the right."

25th Near Beauvais, Adolf Hitler met with the French naval commander François Darlan. Hitler was in a foul mood and declared he was offering military collaboration with Vichy France one last time, and if France refused again it would be "one of the most regrettable decisions in her history."

29th Superman co-creator Joe Shuster was arrested in Miami Beach, Florida for the "suspicious behaviour" of looking into an automobile as if preparing to steal it. The following day he was sentenced to 30 days in prison until someone thought to give Shuster a pen and paper so he could prove his identity. Shuster drew a perfect illustration of Superman and the police let him go free.

30th The famous photograph St Paul's Survives was taken of St Paul's Cathedral in London during the Second Great Fire of London.

31st RAF bombers attacked Vlorë on the Greco-Italian front, Rotterdam and IJmuiden in the Nazi-occupied Netherlands, and the German cities of Emmerich am Rhein and Cologne.

Hitler issued a New Year's Order of the Day to Germany's armed forces, declaring "the year 1941 will bring us, on the Western Front, the completion of the greatest victory of our history."

PEOPLE IN POWER

Robert Menzies
1939-1941
Australia
Prime Minister

Philippe Pétain
1940-1944
France
Président

Getúlio Vargas
1930-1945
Brazil
President

William Mackenzie King
1935-1948
Canada
Prime Minister

Lin Sen
1931-1943
China
Government of China

Adolf Hitler
1934-1945
Germany
Führer of Germany

Marquess of Linlithgow
1936-1943
India
Viceroy of India

Benito Mussolini
1922-19543
Italy
President

Hiroito
1926-1989
Japan
Emperor

Manuel Ávila Camacho
1940-1946
Mexico
President

Joseph Stalin
1922-1952
Russia
Premier

Jan Smuts
1939-1948
South Africa
Prime Minister

Franklin D. Roosevelt
1933-1945
United States
President

Hubert Pierlot
1939-1945
Belgium
Prime Minister

Peter Fraser
1939-1949
New Zealand
Prime Minister

Sir Winston Churchill
1940-1945
United Kingdom
Prime Minister

Per Albin Hansson
1936-1946
Sweden
Prime Minister

Christian X
1912-1947
Denmark
King

Francisco Franco
1936-1975
Spain
President

Miklós Horthy
1920-1944
Hungary
Kingdom of Hungary

The Year You Were Born 1940
Book by Sapphire Publishing

Printed in Great Britain
by Amazon